Devoted to Prayer

Marshall McDaniel

ONE STONE
BIBLICAL RESOURCES

Devoted to Prayer

Scripture quotations taken from the New American Standard Bible® (NASB),
Copyright © 1960, 1962, 1963, 1968, 1971, 1972, 1973, 1975, 1977, 1995
by The Lockman Foundation
Used by permission. www.Lockman.org

Design by Stephen Sebree / Moonlight Graphic Works

Published by One Stone Press
979 Lovers Lane
Bowling Green, KY 42103

Printed in the United States of America

ISBN-13: 978-1-941422-50-2

ONESTONE
BIBLICAL RESOURCES

Contents

Acknowledgements 4

Introduction 5

Part 1: Know

Lesson 1: The Foundation of Prayer Is God 9

Lesson 2: God Knows Everything We Need 13

Lesson 3: Nothing Is Too Hard for God 17

Lesson 4: God Listens to Prayer Everywhere 21

Lesson 5: Grace Makes Prayer Possible 25

Lesson 6: God Take Pleasure in Our Prayers 29

Lesson 7: Approaching God with Reverence 33

Lesson 8: More Than Academic 37

Part 2: Believe

Lesson 9: No Faith, No Prayer 43

Lesson 10: God Is Trustworthy 47

Lesson 11: The Essential Link Between Prayer and Bible Study 51

Lesson 12: Prayer Is "Risky" 55

Lesson 13: Faith Changes Our Focus 59

Lesson 14: How Do We Pray in Faith? (Part 1: What It Doesn't Mean) 63

Lesson 15: How Do We Pray in Faith? (Part 2: What It Does Mean) 67

Lesson 16: Prayer Proves Our Faith 71

Part 3: Engage

Lesson 17: Prayer Requires Discipline 77

Lesson 18: We Must Dedicate Time to Prayer 81

Lesson 19: The Kinds of Prayers God Rewards 85

Lesson 20: Praying Different Kinds of Prayers (Part 1) 89

Lesson 21: Praying Different Kinds of Prayers (Part 2) 93

Lesson 22: How Can We Pray More Passionately? 97

Lesson 23: Evangelistic Prayer 101

Lesson 24: A Lifelong Commitment Is a Daily Decision 105

Appendix 1: Staying Focused in Prayer 108

Appendix 2: Let the People Say "Amen" 110

Appendix 3: Prayer and Fasting 112

Appendix 4: Praying in the Holy Spirit 114

Appendix 5: Calling on the Name of the Lord 116

Works Consulted 117

Acknowledgements

This workbook brings together the ideas of several individuals. Many have been involved at various stages of development. These deserve special recognition: While I was working with the Perry Hill Road church of Christ in Montgomery, Alabama, Rodger Cobia, one of the elders, originated the idea of an extended study of prayer. John Demas then suggested that knowing God must be the prerequisite of effective prayer. Through their individual recommendations, the arrangement of the entire workbook was conceived. They, along with others—including my wife Emily, my father Ken McDaniel, my brother Colton McDaniel, and my sister-in-Christ Kate Williams—edited much of the material. My appreciation also goes to Stephen Sebree who designed the workbook and offered helpful suggestions throughout the process and to Andy Alexander and One Stone Press for publishing the material. I also want to acknowledge my brothers and sisters at the Perry Hill Road church of Christ who first studied this workbook in its entirety. Their patience, encouragement, and advice were invaluable. And last but certainly not least, I give thanks for my wife Emily, my sons Caleb, Noah, Joel, and my daughter Elizabeth. Their unconditional love and continual support give me strength for today and hope for tomorrow.

Introduction

Excellent resources are already available on the subject of prayer, supplying students with helpful and practical information. Why, then, add another workbook to the mix? This study, approaches the subject with a different goal. Its focus is not knowledge of prayer but commitment to it. It seems that most of us struggle more with the latter than the former. This study is a motivational guide to help us become devoted to prayer (see Acts 2:42; Romans 12:12; Colossians 4:2).

This workbook is organized around the following words: *know, believe*, and *engage*. These concepts ought to describe our devotion to God in prayer and all other spiritual endeavors. Only when we come to know God (Part 1) and believe in Him (Part 2) will we have reason to pray and find pleasure in it. Then will we engage God in prayer (Part 3).

Each part of this workbook contains eight lessons, for a total of twenty-four, designed to be completed in twelve weeks. Additional topics are provided in the appendices for those on a thirteen-week schedule. For groups that can only meet once a week, I suggest the following arrangement—Lessons 1, 2, 6, 7, 8, 10, 11, 15, 16, 17, 19, 22, and 24.

This study presents biblical examples of real people who struggled and succeeded in prayer and contains individual and group discussion questions for personal evaluation and collective edification. Other suggested activities include the "Pray" and "Sing" sections. The prayer suggestions are not designed to limit the content of our prayers but to offer helpful guidance to those who are just beginning a prayer habit. A specific amount of time in prayer is also proposed. If the time recommendation is followed, by the end of the study, participants will be praying for a total of fifteen minutes daily. The "Sing" sections focus on important themes in the lessons and are designed for personal and collective use. The written content of each lesson has been intentionally limited to shorter, conversational readings to encourage student completion.

Ultimately, only God, His word, and individual commitment can radically change your prayer life, but perhaps this workbook can point you to Him, highlight His word, and motivate greater devotion. If you are ready to know God better, to believe Him fully, and to engage Him in prayer—in other words, to be devoted to prayer—let's get started.

Marshall McDaniel, 2019

PART 1

KNOW

LESSON 1

The Foundation of Prayer Is God

Every religion possesses some form of human-divine interaction called prayer. The English word is defined as "special communion with a god or some other object of worship." The prayers of Christians are unique, because they are based on the supernatural revelation of the one, true God. Because prayer originates from God, we know that it is pleasing to Him.

God invites us to seek Him in prayer. He tells us that He is near and wants to be found by us (see Isaiah 55:6). He asks us to bring our petitions to Him, "casting all [our] anxieties on Him, because He cares for [us]" (1 Peter 5:7). Simply stated, God longs for us to interact with Him in prayer. However, our interaction with God needs to be understood correctly. We need to distinguish between communication from God (revelation) and communication to God (prayer).

- God-initiated communication is best labeled "revelation." In the Bible, God sometimes spoke directly to people. He initiated the interaction, and they responded (see Genesis 3:9–19; 4:9–15). Yet their responses were not prayer, per se.
- Human-initiated communication is often called "prayer." The first "prayer" in the Bible is described as calling on the name of the Lord (Genesis 4:26). (The action of calling on the name of the Lord, no doubt, involves much more than simply praying. See Appendix 5.)

In sum, God engages us by revelation, and we engage God by prayer. We will, therefore, use the following definition in our study: Prayer is the human-initiated, divinely approved method of communicating with God.

Yet knowing a definition of prayer and recognizing that God wants us to pray are not the only prerequisites for praying effectively. Since we have separated ourselves from God, our sins must first be removed. Otherwise, God will not listen. The Bible says, "Behold, the LORD's hand is not so short / That it cannot save; / Nor is His ear dull / That it cannot hear. / But your iniquities have made a separation between you and your God, / And your sins have hidden His face from you so that He does not hear" (Isaiah 59:1–2). In such a condition, we would likely not pray appropriately anyway (see Jeremiah 17:9; Proverbs 14:12).

Is communication with God even possible? It is! But only if our relationship with God is renewed and restored, something that only happens when we know God and are known by Him (see Galatians 4:9). (We will discuss this concept in detail in Lesson 5.) However, knowing God is not just knowing some things about God. Knowing God is a relational concept. It implies not only fellowship but interaction. Prayer is an important part, but is not the only part.

Our communication with God is not one-sided. It involves, as indicated above, both speaking (prayer) and listening (revelation). The Bible is God's self-revelation, allowing us to come to know Him as He really is (Lesson 6). The Bible is God's autobiography. He tells us about Himself—His nature, His characteristics, His will. When we read, a beautiful cycle begins: we come to know God better through His word, and that changes our prayers to Him. Then, as our prayer life is transformed, our relationship with God deepens, which drives us back to the Scriptures. In this way, God is the foundation of prayer.

God invites us to pray to Him. He accepts our prayers. He enables us to pray. Knowledge of Him enlivens our prayers. We choose to acknowledge Him every time we pray. Only then can we express our deepest sentiments and glorify Him. When our prayers are based on the knowledge of God, they evidence a deeper, mature spiritual focus (see Matthew 26:39, 42).

In Part 1 ("Know"), we will concentrate on God—who He is, what He does, and what He longs to do for us—with the intention of knowing Him as He is. This will help us to be more devoted to prayer.

Pray

Try to commit to at least four minutes of prayer daily this week. Consider beginning with these prayer suggestions.

- **Week 1, Day 1:** Thank God that He has provided you with the privilege of prayer.
- **Week 1, Day 2:** Ask God to give you a heart that longs to know Him authentically and intimately.
- **Week 1, Day 3:** Praise God for what you already know about Him.
- **Week 1, Day 4:** Promise God that you will seek to know Him in a deeper, more meaningful way.

Sing

"Nearer, Still Nearer," Leila Morris

Examine

Do I have a mature or immature relationship with God? Why? How is my present knowledge of God affecting my prayers to Him? What can I do today to deepen my understanding of God and my relationship with Him?

_____

_____

_____

_____

Discuss

Answer the following questions. Be ready to discuss them as a group.

1. When you use the word *prayer*, what do you mean? Why is prayer important to you? Do you feel like prayer is a priority in your life? Explain. Describe a time when prayer (public or private) was especially meaningful to you.

_____

_____

_____

_____

2. Has anyone ever possessed greater knowledge of God than Jesus Christ? Did His understanding of God lead Him to pray more or less? With greater fervency or less? Why do you think that is? Provide biblical examples.

_____

_____

_____

_____

3. In what way(s) does God reveal Himself to us? How has growing in your knowledge of God changed your prayers? What characteristics of God cause you to pray to Him more often and more fervently?

_____

_____

_____

_____

LESSON 2

God Knows Everything We Need

We've probably heard it before. Perhaps we've even said it ourselves. "If God knows everything, then why should I pray?" That is an important question.

The Bible affirms that God is all-knowing (omniscient). As the psalmist writes, "Great is our Lord and abundant in strength; / His understanding is infinite" (Psalm 147:5). So if God is omniscient, then isn't it unreasonable that He demand something of us that He already knows? Prayer becomes an empty ritual, right? No, God is not being unreasonable, and prayer is not vain. How do we know this?

The omniscience of God—along with His gracious providence—should motivate us to pray (see Matthew 6:8). The foreknowledge of God does not force Him to be rigid and unmoved by our prayers (see 2 Samuel 21:14). While it is true that there are certain plans and purposes of God that cannot be changed, the Bible tells us that prayer is effective and that it accomplishes what God desires (see James 5:16). God listens to prayers and sometimes moves in a different direction because of them (see Numbers 21:6–9; 2 Kings 20:1–11). This does not mean that God is unsure of Himself or His plans, vacillating at the whims of those who pray to Him. Rather, when God responds to our prayers, He is exercising His sovereign right to do so, and all His responses manifest abundant grace. (More on this in Lesson 5.) For prayer to be effective, we must come to know God as the all-knowing One.

What happens to us and our prayers when we appreciate the omniscience of God?

First, appreciating the omniscience of God boosts our confidence in Him and in the effectiveness of prayer. How God answers our prayers is frequently beyond our finite understanding, but that He does provide what is best, responding with "Yes" to many of our requests, cannot be disputed. The apostle John was so convinced that God answers prayer that he wrote, "This is the confidence which we have before Him, that if we ask anything according to His will, He hears us. And if we know that He hears us in whatever we ask, we know that we have the requests which we have asked Him" (1 John 5:14–15). What an amazing promise! Though God knows exactly what we need, He still longs to hear our requests.

Second, the omniscience of God leads us to pray more. Since God knows everything we need before we ask, we believe that He always gives the best answer to our prayers—though that sometimes does not match what we want (Lesson 15). Furthermore, if we do not ask or if we ask with selfish motives, we should not expect to receive anything from Him (see James 4:2–3). Knowing God as He really is—the omniscient God—compels us to bring our requests to Him unselfishly and in line with His revealed will (Lesson 13).

Third, knowing that God is all-knowing brings personal peace. Our anxieties and fears lose their grip in the light of His infinite understanding, and our faith and hope in God are strengthened. The Bible says, "Be anxious for nothing, but in everything by prayer and supplication with thanksgiving let your requests be made known to God. And the peace of God, which surpasses all comprehension, will guard your hearts and your minds in Christ Jesus" (Philippians 4:6–7; see 1 Peter 5:7). God's all-knowing nature, His gracious providence, and our confident prayers come together to provide true, divine peace. Isn't that the kind of peace that we ultimately desire?

The all-knowing nature of God, instead of discouraging prayer, gives us every reason to pray. He knows our needs; He knows our requests; and He always gives us what is best. What wonderful reasons to pray fervently to God today!

Pray

Try to commit to at least four minutes of prayer daily this week. Consider beginning with these prayer suggestions.

- **Week 1, Day 5:** Praise God that He knows everything.
- **Week 1, Day 6:** Thank God for listening to your prayers and for His gracious answers.
- **Week 1, Day 7:** Ask God to grant your specific requests. (Consider making a prayer list before praying.)

Sing

"Are You Weighed Down?" Craig Roberts

Examine

Have I ever used the excuse that God knows everything to pray less (or stop praying altogether)? If so, how strong was my relationship with God at that point? If not, have I ever failed to pray because I felt my request was too insignificant for an all-knowing God? If I really believe that God knows everything I need, what bold request should I make of Him today?

_____

_____

_____

_____

Discuss

Answer the following questions. Be ready to discuss them as a group.

1. Read Matthew 6:5–15. What was the problem with the prayers of the Gentiles, and what characteristic of God prevents His people from praying like them? How does the Model Prayer of Jesus demonstrate a mature understanding of the all-knowing nature of God? How will knowing that God is omniscient change our prayers?

_____

_____

_____

_____

2. Does God need us to pray to Him? Why, or why not? Why do you think God asks us to pray?

_____

_____

_____

_____

3. Read Philippians 4:6–7. What is the peace of God, and in what way(s) does it guard our hearts and minds? Can you think of a time when you determined not to worry about something, prayed about it, and experienced the peace of God? If so, be ready to share your experience with others.

_____

_____

_____

_____

LESSON 3 — Nothing Is Too Hard for God

There are two kinds of atheists: professed atheists and practical atheists. Professed atheists deny the possibility of anything or anyone supernatural. Practical atheists, on the other hand, verbally acknowledge the existence of God but act as if God is limited or inactive. Titus 1:16 describes practical atheists in this way: "They profess to know God, but by their deeds they deny Him, being detestable and disobedient and worthless for any good deed." Both forms of atheism are flawed and ultimately undermine our relationship with God.

God has made it abundantly clear that He exists and that he can do anything He wants to do. How do we know God is all-powerful?

- God created the universe and everything in it (see Genesis 1:1; 2:7; Psalm 33:6; Romans 1:20).
- God miraculously delivered His people from Egyptian slavery and providentially cared for them throughout their history (see Exodus 15:1–13; 20:2; Deuteronomy 5:15).
- God brought His Son into this world and after the crucifixion resurrected Him to everlasting life (see Luke 1:31–37; Acts 10:38; Romans 1:3–4).
- God revealed and confirmed His word, resulting in a compelling, indestructible, and saving message for the world (see Hebrews 2:1–4; Romans 1:16–17; 2 Timothy 3:16–17).

No wonder God asks this rhetorical question, "Is anything too difficult for Me?" (Jeremiah 32:27). Nothing is too hard for God! What we see as impossible does not intimidate God. He is not limited by our flawed human perspective or by our weaknesses (see Matthew 19:26; Luke 1:37). He "is able to do far more abundantly beyond all that we ask or think" (Ephesians 3:20).

God wants us to experience His power (omnipotence). The expanded phrase in Ephesians 3:20 reads, "[He] is able to do far more abundantly beyond all that we ask or think according to the power that works within us." He has made His omnipotence available to us and intends to work mightily within us (see Philippians 2:13; Colossians 1:29).

How do we experience God's power? One way is through prayer. The Bible says, "The effective prayer of a righteous man can accomplish much" (James 5:16). This does not mean that simply knowing what to say in prayer and how to say it makes prayer effective (see Matthew 6:5–8). Instead, it is a relationship with God Almighty that makes it work. Only when we come to God humbly, recognizing His ability and our weaknesses, can we experience His power. Paul highlights the connection between prayer, divine omnipotence, and human frailty in 2 Corinthians 12:9: "And [the Lord] said to me, 'My grace is sufficient for you, for power is perfected in weakness.' Most gladly, therefore, I will rather boast about my weaknesses, so that the power of Christ may dwell in me." Prayer connects us to the power of God, regardless of whether we receive an affirmative answer to our requests.

Do we really know God as God Almighty? Or are we practical atheists who deny God and His power, praying small and few prayers? Hopefully we are not like those in the following fictional story popularized on social media:

A man obtained a permit to open the first tavern in a small town. The members of a local church were strongly opposed to the bar, so they began to openly pray that God would intervene. A few days before the tavern opened, lightning struck the structure and burned it to the ground. The people of the church were surprised but pleased, that is, until they received notice that the tavern owner was suing them. He contended that their prayers were responsible for the destruction of his building. They denied the charge. After the preliminary hearing, the judge wryly remarked, "At this point I don't know what my decision will be, but it seems that the tavern owner believes in the power of prayer and the church people do not."

It is doubtful that God wants us to pray for the destruction of property, but the story teaches an important lesson. A lack of faith in the power of God will affect our view of prayer. What is the solution to this problem? Know God as He is—God Almighty—and pray to Him accordingly.

Pray

Try to commit to at least five minutes of prayer daily this week. Consider beginning with these prayer suggestions.

- **Week 2, Day 1:** Praise God for His all-powerful nature.
- **Week 2, Day 2:** Ask God to help you to know Him as God Almighty.
- **Week 2, Day 3:** Thank God for the ways He has demonstrated His power in your life.
- **Week 2, Day 4:** Ask God for help with something that you absolutely cannot accomplish on your own. (Be specific.)

Sing

"How Great Thou Art," Stewart Hine

Examine

Do I ever question the all-powerful nature of God? If so, when do I have an especially difficult time accepting that God is all-powerful? Is there anything that I have failed to request of God, because I thought it impossible? If so, what? (Consider asking God for it now.)

_____

_____

_____

_____

Discuss

Answer the following questions. Be ready to discuss them as a group.

1. What are ways in which God has demonstrated that He is all-powerful? (Provide biblical examples. Be specific.) If God has proven His ability, why do we sometimes doubt that He will help us? What should we do when we find ourselves doubting God's power?

_____

_____

_____

_____

_____

_____

2. Read 2 Corinthians 12:7–10. Does God want us to experience His power? God often perfects His power in us when we are in what condition? Even though God said "No" to Paul's request, did this negatively affect Paul's view of God? Explain.

_____

_____

_____

_____

3. Read 1 John 5:14–15 and James 5:13–18. Though the omnipotence of God is not specifically mentioned in these passages, what phrases assume that God is all-powerful? What kinds of issues are we to bring to God in prayer? When we know that God's power is unlimited, how will it affect our prayers?

_____

_____

_____

_____

LESSON 4

God Listens to Prayer Everywhere

Psalm 139 is one of the most majestic songs in the Bible. It acknowledges the greatness of God—His omniscience (Lesson 2) and His omnipotence (Lesson 3). It also highlights another divine characteristic that, like the others, is beyond our limited comprehension—God's omnipresence. The psalmist asks, "Where can I go from Your Spirit? / Or where can I flee from Your presence?" (v. 7). The answer to these questions is obvious: nowhere. We cannot escape the presence of God. If we ascend on high, He is there; if we cover ourselves in the depths of the earth, He is there; and even if we could travel at the speed of light, we could not hide ourselves from Him (see vv. 8–10). He is present everywhere simultaneously.

The concept of omnipresence is difficult—if not impossible—for us to grasp. Omnipresence does not mean that God is somehow being physically stretched throughout the universe; He is not limited by space and time as we are. God, as an infinite spiritual being, is capable of being equally present in every place without being confined to any single location (see John 4:24; Jeremiah 23:23–24).

The ever-present nature of God means that He is transcendent, separate from and above this physical, natural universe. However, the omnipresence of God also implies that He is immanent. He is, in a sense, always near (see Acts 17:27–28). Yet God longs for an even closer relationship with us, taking His universal nearness to another level—a spiritual connection. God's promise in 2 Corinthians 6:16 expresses this desire. God says, "I will dwell in [you] and walk among [you]; / And I will be [your] God, and [you] shall be My people" (see also Leviticus 26:12). That is the level of intimacy God wants.

What about us? Do we long for a close relationship with God? The Bible encourages us to "seek the LORD while He may be found" and to "call upon Him while He is near" (Isaiah 55:6). So how do we connect with God? Prayer. This is, of course, not the only step, but it is an essential one. No relationship—human or divine—can thrive apart from communication.

Prayer is like and unlike other forms of human communication.

- Prayer is *like* other forms of communication in that God is, in a very real sense, present with us. We can speak with Him freely and directly.
- Prayer is *unlike* other forms of communication in that the presence of God is spiritual, and our communication with Him must be spiritual.

God specifically promised His people of old, "Then you will call upon Me and come and pray to Me, and I will listen to you. You will seek Me and find Me when you search for Me with all your heart. I will be found by you" (Jeremiah 29:12–14). God is not out of reach. He is near, He wants to be found, and prayer connects us to Him.

Does the omnipresence of God encourage us? Or does it intimidate us? The answer to these questions probably depends on our present relationship with Him (see Psalm 139:17–22). Regardless of our current connection—strong, weak, or non-existent—God is listening and ready to actively work in our lives—if we will open ourselves up to Him (see Philippians 2:12–13). Like the psalmist, perhaps we should start with a prayer like this: "Search me, O God, and know my heart; / Try me and know my anxious thoughts; / And see if there be any hurtful way in me, / And lead me in the everlasting way" (Psalm 139:23–24; see Hebrews 4:13). This is an essential step toward experiencing the bliss of a close relationship with the omnipresent Lord.

If you are not yet a Christian, God will listen to your plea to have a relationship with Him, but He expects you to hear and obey His word to become His child (see Acts 10:1–8, 24–48; Appendix 5). Will you take the initial step today?

Pray

Try to commit to at least five minutes of prayer daily this week. Consider beginning with these prayer suggestions.

- **Week 2, Day 5:** Thank God for always being close to you.
- **Week 2, Day 6:** Promise God that you will draw near to Him, developing a deeper spiritual connection.
- **Week 2, Day 7:** Ask God to search your heart, to reveal anything that is harming your relationship with Him, and to guide you in the right way.

Sing

"Be with Me, Lord," Thomas Chisholm

Examine

Does the omnipresence of God encourage me? Why, or why not? Is there anything that is preventing me from having a close relationship with God? What can I do to draw closer to Him today?

_____

_____

_____

_____

Discuss

Answer the following questions. Be ready to discuss them as a group.

1. Read Acts 17:24–28. What phrases in this reading indicate that God is not confined to our universe? What limitations do we possess that make it difficult for us to grasp the omnipresence of God?

_____

_____

_____

_____

2. Read Psalm 139. The attributes of God—omniscience, omnipresence, omnipotence, holiness—affect people in diverse ways. What differing attitudes and actions characterize the wicked and the righteous in Psalm 139? How does God want us to respond to Him, and what has He promised His people? (see Jeremiah 29:11–14)

_____

_____

_____

_____

3. How might knowing that God is omnipresent affect our personal and collective prayers? (Consider the aspects of prayer that could be affected: how we pray, what we pray, where we pray, when we pray, and why we pray.)

_____

_____

_____

_____

Grace Makes Prayer Possible

The hymn "Amazing Grace" is one of the most recognizable songs in the English-speaking world today. Though the popular tune ("New Britain") was not attached to the lyrics until 1835, the famous words have been sung again and again since John Newton first published them in 1779. The lyrics magnify grace as that which saves, instructs, encourages, and protects. Truly, the grace of God is amazing! But what is grace, and how is it connected to prayer?

Grace is typically defined as "unmerited favor." Yet this description is somewhat simplistic, since the Bible describes the grace of God as manifold ("varied, diverse, or multifaceted," see 1 Peter 4:10). Even though grace is a deep concept, it is foundational, at the very heart

of our relationship with God. For our purposes, we will define *grace* as "the good pleasure of God that inclines Him to bestow benefits upon the undeserving" (A. W. Tozer).

God wants to give good gifts to His people. Why? Because He is good! The psalmists accurately describe God, saying, "You are good and do good," and "The LORD gives grace and glory; / No good thing does He withhold from those who walk uprightly" (Psalms 119:68; 84:11; see Acts 14:16–17). We need grace to envelop our lives. Apart from God, we cannot experience good.

Our need for grace is clearly recognizable in view of our sinfulness (see Ephesians 2:1–3). Sometimes we may trick ourselves into thinking we are good people, but God breaks through our self-deception and shows just how bad we are and how much we need His grace and love (see 2:4–9). The Bible affirms that "all have sinned and fall short of the glory of God" (Romans 3:23). We are sinners, and we will never see our need for grace until we come to terms with our own wretchedness (see Romans 7:24).

Sin is an impenetrable barrier between us and God. God is holy and just. We cannot approach Him as sinners: "Behold, the LORD's hand is not so short / That it cannot save; / Nor is His ear so dull / That it cannot hear. / But your iniquities have made a separation between you and your God, / And your sins have hidden His face from you so that He does not hear" (Isaiah 59:1–2). God will not even listen to our prayers when we openly reject Him (see Micah 3:4; Proverbs 28:9).

Yet God is gracious! The Bible says, "For His anger is but for a moment, / His favor is for a lifetime; / Weeping may last for the night, / But a shout of joy comes in the morning" (Psalm 30:5). Grace makes the human-divine relationship possible because it breaks down the barriers that we have erected between ourselves and God. Grace saves us from our sin-cursed condition: "For by grace you have been saved through faith; and that not of yourselves, it is the gift of God" (Ephesians 2:8; see 1:7; Romans 6:23).

Grace creates a new relationship. God becomes our Father, and we His children (see Galatians 3:26–28; Romans 8:14–17; Ephesians 1:3–6). As such, we can freely approach Him in prayer, discovering grace over and over again: "Therefore let us draw near with confidence to the throne of grace, so that we may receive mercy and find grace to help in time of need" (Hebrews 4:16; see Matthew 6:9–13). God's grace makes prayer possible.

Have *you* received His grace? Now is the time. Salvation is by grace, but it is also *through* faith (see Ephesians 2:8–9). We need the grace of God, but we must believe to receive it (see Part 2). Will you accept God's grace today?

Amazing grace, how sweet the sound
That saved a wretch like me!
I once was lost, but now I'm found,
Was blind, but now I see.

Pray

Try to commit to at least six minutes of prayer daily this week. Consider beginning with these prayer suggestions.

- **Week 3, Day 1:** Praise and thank God for His amazing grace.
- **Week 3, Day 2:** Confess to God any sin(s) that is creating a barrier between you and Him.
- **Week 3, Day 3:** Ask God to manifest His grace in your life and to help you to be more aware of His grace.
- **Week 3, Day 4:** Promise God that you will learn from His grace, remove the evil from your life, and pursue the good.

Sing

"Amazing Grace," John Newton

Examine

When I think about God, do I truly believe that He is gracious? In what way(s) has God shown me that He is good and that He wants what is best for me? Does my present understanding of the grace of God cause me to ignore my sins or to turn from them? (see Romans 6:1–7; Titus 2:11–14)

_____

_____

_____

_____

Discuss

Answer the following questions. Be ready to discuss them as a group.

1. Read Psalm 107. It begins with "Oh give thanks to the LORD, for He is good, / For His lovingkindness is everlasting" (v. 1). In what way(s) does Psalm 107 demonstrate that God is gracious? Describe a time in your life when the grace of God was especially real and meaningful to you.

_____

_____

_____

_____

2. Look carefully at the lyrics to "Amazing Grace." Why do you think "Amazing Grace" has become so popular? From the hymn, what are some of the descriptions and actions associated with grace? (Optional Assignment: Find the Bible passages that inspired the lyrics of the hymn.)

_____

_____

_____

_____

3. Why (and how) does sin hinder and discourage prayer? (Provide biblical and personal examples.) How does grace enable and encourage prayer?

_____

_____

_____

_____

LESSON 6

God Takes Pleasure in Our Prayers

A. W. Tozer affirms that "we tend by a secret law of the soul to move toward our mental image of God." If true—and it seems to be—it is indeed dangerous to think low thoughts of God. When we reject God as He is or try to reduce Him, we risk becoming like those described in Romans 1:21: "futile in [our] speculations" and "[our] heart [being] darkened." Our relationship with God and our dedication to prayer are dependent on our knowledge of Him.

Do we see God as He really is? Or are we simply seeing what we want to see?

How sad that many people—sometimes even Christians—live and pray in a way that demonstrates ignorance of God. Some seem to act as if God is distant and annoyed with them, that He is a cosmic bully, a cold politician, or a critical parent. Why would anyone want to pray to such a God?! That is not God at all! Those images are false, imaginary gods. Worshiping those false images is idolatrous. J. I. Packer writes that while modern men and women have typically abandoned "molten images" of God, they frequently pick up false "mental images" of Him and slip into the idolatry of old. Like molten images, false mental images of God will always disappoint us; praying to God as if these are valid representations of His nature will eventually deform and destroy us (see Isaiah 44:9; 45:20; Psalm 115:4–8).

Praise God that He is not distant and annoyed with us and that He is not lifeless and inept! He is real, He is alive, and He wants us to reach out to Him—especially in prayer (see Acts 17:24–29). God enjoys hearing us pray to Him (see Proverbs 15:8). How do we know this?

First, God has shown us that He is intimately concerned with our welfare. God did not create us simply to leave us to our own devices. Rather, He constantly demonstrates His steadfast love for us (Lesson 5). Psalm 107 fittingly describes various groups of people who called on the Lord and experienced His mercy. God satisfied the hungry (vv. 4–9), freed the captives (vv. 10–16), healed the afflicted (vv. 17–22), and quieted the anxious (vv. 23–32). They called, and He answered. God truly cares about people and enjoys granting their requests.

Second, God has clearly demonstrated through His Son Jesus Christ that He loves us and wants to connect with us. The Bible says, "But God demonstrates His own love toward us, in that while we were yet sinners, Christ died for us. Much more then, having now been justified by His blood, we shall be saved from the wrath of God through Him" (Romans 5:8; see John 3:16). We can approach God as children because of Jesus Christ. Now, in Christ, we know with certainty that He longs to hear and answer our prayers (see Matthew 7:7–11).

Our prayers bring God great pleasure. The Bible says, "The sacrifice of the wicked is an abomination to the LORD, / But the prayer of the upright is His delight" (Proverbs 15:8). The contrast between sacrifice and prayer is striking. While the wicked offered superficial "worship" to God, the righteous fulfilled the requirement of God's law from their heart, offering up earnest prayers with their sacrifices (see Hosea 6:6; Psalm 51:15–17). If we have been justified by God, our prayers are favorable to Him and accepted by Him. God loves to hear the prayers of his saints (see Proverbs 15:29).

Is it our goal to please God? (see 2 Corinthians 5:9). If it is, we must bring our mental image of God into conformity with what God has revealed about Himself in the Bible. We need to see God as He really is—a God who loves to hear our prayers. Then—and only then—can we be devoted to prayer and "continually offer up a sacrifice of praise to God, that is, the fruit of lips that give thanks to His name" (Hebrews 13:15; see 1 Thessalonians 5:17).

Pray

Try to commit to at least six minutes of prayer daily this week. Consider beginning with these prayer suggestions.

- **Week 3, Day 5:** Ask God to help you identify and eliminate any false mental images of Him that you have created in your mind.
- **Week 3, Day 6:** Thank God for loving you and listening to your prayers.
- **Week 3, Day 7:** Promise God that you will be more devoted to prayer, especially since that is what pleases Him.

Sing

"**I Close My Eyes,**" Jay Conner

Examine

Do I ever feel like God doesn't love me or that He doesn't care to listen to my prayers? If so, what circumstances lead to these feelings? Is there something that I can change to avoid these doubts? What has helped me to overcome similar challenges in the past?

_____

_____

_____

_____

Discuss

Answer the following questions. Be ready to discuss them as a group.

1. Read Romans 1:18–32. What happens when we exchange the true image of God for false ones? What strategies does Satan use that cause us to doubt that God really loves us? What do we need to do to stand firm against Satan?

_____

_____

_____

_____

2. Read Matthew 7:7–11 and Luke 11:9–13. What phrases in these passages indicate that God loves to hear and answer our prayers? Provide biblical and personal examples of occasions when prayers were offered and God granted the requests.

_____

_____

_____

_____

3. Read Proverbs 15:8. Compare the prayers of the wicked and the upright. Why does God delight in the prayers of the upright? Why should we be concerned whether we bring God pleasure? (see 2 Corinthians 5:9–10) Why do false images prevent us from pleasing God?

_____

_____

_____

_____

LESSON 7
Approaching God with Reverence

God is awesome. The Bible says, "Holy and *awesome* is His name" (Psalm 111:9). The word *awesome* is majestic, especially when it is used as a description of God. Yet the meaning of the English word awesome has changed in recent years. At one time, it was almost exclusively associated with "apprehension," "fear," and "admiration." Close synonyms included *terrible, dreadful, fearful,* and *awful* (see KJV, Psalm 68:35; Daniel 9:4; Exodus 15:11). In most cases, awesome was reserved for God and His works.

Awesome is rarely used in this way today. Frequently, it expresses mere personal interest in a matter. This shift in language is not as troubling as the apparent cultural changes that we see around us (and sometimes among us!) toward irreverence. It seems that people are generally becoming more and more like those so described in the Scriptures: "There is no fear of God before their eyes" (Psalm 36:1; Romans 3:18). Sadly, this applies to both the irreligious and the religious. The corrupt and casual society in which we live sorely needs a restoration of proper reverence for God.

How is irreverence expressed? An illustration is found in Leviticus 10:1–3, when the priests Nadab and Abihu offered incense with unauthorized fire:

> Now Nadab and Abihu, the sons of Aaron, took their respective firepans, and after putting fire in them, placed incense on it and offered strange fire before the LORD, which He had not commanded them. And fire came out from the presence of the LORD and consumed them, and they died before the LORD. Then Moses said to Aaron, "It is what the LORD spoke, saying, 'By those who come near Me I will be treated as holy, / And before all the people I will be honored.'" So Aaron, therefore, kept silent.

The punishment of Nadab and Abihu shows us that God and His will must be respected. To deny the will of God and substitute our own dishonors Him. If our worship—including prayer—does not match what God wants, He views it as an act of irreverence and hypocrisy (see Isaiah 29:13; Mark 7:6–8; John 4:23–24). Worship is not a game. It is serious.

So while worship (e.g. prayer) is to be intimate, it must never be *casual*. The word casual is defined in a variety of ways. Most of these definitions we

would not want to describe our prayers. These include "unconcerned," "irregular," and "accidental." Casual prayer is inappropriate and unworthy of the God to whom we are praying. When some flippantly address God, "Hey, Pops! How's it going today?" they are treading in dangerous territory. God has adopted us as His own children, and we can pray very personal prayers to Him; but God is still God, and we must come before Him with reverence (see Hebrews 12:28–29). Some appeal to the use of *abba* as vindication for being casual with God, but while *abba* is indeed an intimate paternal term, it is by no means a casual one (see Mark 14:36; Romans 8:15; Galatians 4:6).

What characteristics of God make Him worthy of our utmost reverence and respect?

- God is holy. When Moses and Isaiah came face to face with the holiness of God, there was no informality whatsoever (see Exodus 3:1–6; Isaiah 6:1–5).
- God is just. Though Jesus has made an intimate relationship with God possible, He has in no way abolished the fear of the Lord. God is still just, and our life must reflect an understanding of this (see Matthew 10:28; Luke 12:4–5).
- God is good. It is not only the "scary" attributes of God that should lead us to fear Him. The goodness of God also demands our respect (see 1 Samuel 12:24; Philippians 2:12–13; Romans 2:4).

Thinking back to Psalm 111, just after the psalmist wrote that the name of God is holy and awesome (v. 9), he said, "The fear of the LORD is the beginning of wisdom" (v. 10). Do we long to have an intimate relationship with God? Developing fear, reverence, and adoration for God is a good starting place. If we do this, God hears us, and that is truly awesome.

Pray

Try to commit to at least seven minutes of prayer daily this week. Consider beginning with these prayer suggestions.

- **Week 4, Day 1:** Praise God, using biblical phrases—like those in Psalm 111—to extol His greatness.
- **Week 4, Day 2:** Ask God to expose irreverent attitudes and habits and to help you respect Him more.
- **Week 4, Day 3:** Promise God that you will not be casual toward Him in word or deed.
- **Week 4, Day 4:** Thank God for His holiness, His justice, His goodness, and any other attributes that cause you to fear and love Him.

Sing

"**I Stand in Awe,**" Mark Altrogge

Examine

What characteristics of God cause me to stand in awe of Him? When I am truly awestruck by God, what are ways by which I can express my adoration for Him? What changes do I need to make in my routine so that I can regularly come "face to face" with the majesty of God?

_____

_____

_____

_____

Discuss

Answer the following questions. Be ready to discuss them as a group.

1. Read Leviticus 10:1–3. Did God overreact in His condemnation of Nadab and Abihu? Why, or why not? In what way(s) do non-believers and believers demonstrate that they do not fear God? Why is irreverence toward God dangerous?

_____

_____

_____

_____

2. Read Hebrews 12:28. This passage indicates that the way we please God is by approaching Him with reverence and awe. Define _reverence_ and _awe_. Compare these terms. How will developing a greater sense of reverence and awe for God affect our service to Him, especially our prayers to Him?

_____

_____

_____

_____

3. "Prayer is intimate, but it must not be casual." Do you agree or disagree with this statement, and why? Why is it sometimes difficult for us to balance intimacy and reverence? How can we develop an appropriate balance between intimacy and reverence?

_____

_____

_____

_____

LESSON 8 More Than Academic

In Part 1 ("Know"), we have examined just a few of the many and manifold characteristics of God. We cannot attain a comprehensive knowledge of God in a few short lessons but we can make it our goal to continue to learn what the Lord has revealed about Himself (see Deuteronomy 29:29). Knowing God is a lifelong pursuit that requires daily interaction with God at the personal and spiritual level (Lesson 24). This is not a burden; it is our greatest privilege (see 1 John 5:3; Jeremiah 9:24). But, to connect with God requires that our knowledge of Him be more than academic.

Wouldn't it be disappointing if we found ourselves approaching Christianity solely from an intellectual perspective? While we should never deny the logical and rational basis of our faith, we need not overreact and deny its other aspects—including the emotional and the physical. While some people seek only emotional experiences to authenticate their "knowledge" of God, this mistake does not deny the importance of a comprehensive love for God. The Greatest Commandment says, "The Lord our God is one Lord; and you shall love the Lord your God with all your heart, and with all your soul, and with all your mind, and with all your strength" (Mark 12:29–30). Our interaction with God should engage every aspect of our being.

For this reason, God does not expect prayer to be simply an intellectual experience. When we pray, there should be feeling. The prayers of the Bible are not dispassionate, repetitive requests; they are fervent, heartfelt pleas. For example, in Ezra 9 and 10, Ezra, a scribe, had intellectual knowledge of God, but it did not stop there; he personalized his relationship with the Lord. Seeing major flaws in himself and the rest of God's people, he prayed passionately and contritely that God would forgive them. The Bible says, "Now while Ezra was praying and making confession, weeping and prostrating himself before the house of God, a very large assembly, men, women, and children, gathered to him from Israel; for the people wept bitterly" (Ezra 10:1). Ezra was not putting on a show. Through prayer, he connected with God, and his heartfelt expression touched others, leading them to do the same.

That is the kind of knowledge we need—not only intellectual knowledge but also personal and emotional knowledge.

So, how do we go about developing a complete knowledge and response to God? It will not happen just because we have been a Christian for a few years. We develop a true knowledge of God by committing to regular study of the Bible, trusting the Lord, and experiencing His goodness (see 1 Peter 2:2–3; Psalm 34:8).

We need to open ourselves up to God in prayer (see Psalm 139:23–24). Prayer is meant to be a deeply personal, spiritual connection with God (see 1 Samuel 1:12–16). The Bible says, "In the same way the Spirit also helps in our weakness; for we do not know how to pray as we should, but the Spirit Himself intercedes for us with groaning too deep for words; and He who searches the hearts knows what the mind of the Spirit is, because He intercedes for the saints according to the will of God" (Romans 8:26–27). We pour out our souls to God in prayer, even when we do not know what to say, and God, through the intercession of the Holy Spirit, knows the sentiments of our hearts. This kind of prayer engages mind and soul, intellect and emotion, knowledge and feeling (see 1 Corinthians 14:15). This kind of prayer touches the heart of God.

Do we feel disconnected from God? Let's not pursue a "quick-fix," a temporary, superficial feeling. Let's seek to know God as He is. When we do, we won't have to try to create feelings; they will be there; and we will be well on our way toward being devoted to prayer.

Pray

Try to commit to at least seven minutes of prayer daily this week. Consider beginning with the following prayer suggestions.

- Week 4, Day 5: Thank God that He allows us to connect with Him through prayer.
- Week 4, Day 6: Ask God to give you a heart that will receive a true knowledge of Him and that will respond appropriately.
- Week 4, Day 7: Promise God that you will make it your daily practice to learn more about Him, to build your relationship with Him, and to pray more passionately to Him.

Sing

"Jesus, Let Us Come to Know You," Michael Card

Examine

Is my relationship with God merely academic? When I pray, do I do so only because intellectually I know I should or because I am also moved by my knowledge of God to speak with Him? What can I do to deepen my understanding of God and my fervency in prayer?

_____

_____

_____

_____

Discuss

Answer the following questions. Be ready to discuss them as a group.

1. Read Mark 12:29–30. Define each of these words: _heart, soul, mind,_ and _strength._ (A Bible dictionary or commentary may prove helpful.) Do these concepts convey only an intellectual devotion to God? Why, or why not?

_____

_____

_____

_____

2. Read Ezra 9–10. What prompted Ezra to pray to God? What words and phrases indicate that Ezra was experiencing strong feelings when he prayed? What was the result of this passionate prayer?

_____

_____

_____

_____

3. Why do we sometimes fail to become emotionally invested in our prayers? What are some of the dangers of disconnecting our emotions from our private and public prayers? What can we do to be more engaged in our relationship with God?

_____

_____

_____

_____

PART 2

BELIEVE

LESSON 9
No Faith, No Prayer

What is faith? Friedrich Nietzsche, a 19th century German philosopher, identified it as "not wanting to know what is true." Some dictionaries include definitions like "belief that does not rest on logical proof or material evidence." The skeptical and the worldly typically label faith in God in similar ways, thinking it foolish to cling to a supposedly irrational belief system. This is an unfair representation of our faith.

Biblical faith is not limited to reason, but it is reasonable. It is undergirded by evidence. Jesus Himself said, "If I do not do the works of My Father, do not believe Me" (John 10:37). He went on to say that we should honestly examine the evidence before dismissing Him (see v. 38). Is there any rationale for faith? There is. For instance,

- Luke investigated the testimonies of the eyewitnesses of Jesus and recorded them in an orderly way. Later, in his second volume (Acts), he showed that Christianity is supported by many convincing proofs (see Luke 1:1–4; Acts 1:1–3).
- Peter shared with his readers some of his experiences, demonstrating that his testimony harmonized with and confirmed the Old Testament prophecies about the Christ (see 2 Peter 1:16–21).
- The apostle John also emphasized his own personal, intimate interaction with the Lord. He affirmed that he had heard, seen, and even touched Jesus (see 1 John 1:1–4).

Biblical faith is not based on unsubstantiated claims. D. Elton Trueblood accurately affirmed that "faith is not belief without proof but trust without reservation." The Bible says, "Trust in the LORD with all your heart / And do not lean on your own understanding. / In all your ways acknowledge Him, / And He will make your paths straight. / Do not be wise in your own eyes; / Fear the LORD and turn away from evil" (Proverbs 3:5–7). This is biblical faith. It is committing ourselves fully to God, appreciating who He is, believing that He knows what is best for us, and doing whatever He tells us to do.

The following real-life story of believers in the Soviet Union, as told by Charles Swindoll, illustrates this kind of faith in action:

One Sunday, a group of believers in the Soviet Union gathered secretly for worship. (Christians had to meet secretly throughout the day so as not to arouse the suspicion of KGB informers.) Suddenly, in walked two soldiers with loaded weapons at the ready. One shouted, "If you wish to renounce your commitment to Jesus Christ, leave now!" Two or three quickly left. Then another. After a few more seconds, two more. "This is your last chance. Either turn against your faith in Christ," the soldier ordered, "or stay and suffer the consequences." Two more slipped out into the night. No one else moved. Parents with children trembling beside them looked down reassuringly, fully expecting to be gunned down or imprisoned. One of the soldiers closed the door, looked back at those who stood against the wall

and said, "Keep your hands up, but this time in praise to our Lord Jesus Christ. We, too, are Christians. We were sent to another house several weeks ago to arrest a group of believers..." The other soldier interrupted, "But, instead, we were converted! We have learned by experience, however, that unless people are willing to die for their faith, they cannot be fully trusted."

Would we do the same?

Our faith may not be tested as intensely as it was for the people in the story, but faith is not only associated with the "big" commitments; it is evidenced by the "small" ones as well, including our prayers. Prayer then is one of the spiritual fruits of trusting God.

If we truly wish to be devoted to prayer, we must learn to trust God. The upcoming lessons will provide suggestions for how to do this, but we can start by cultivating a desire to possess the faith described in Proverbs 3:5–7. When we trust God completely and continually, He will direct us in the right and blessed way.

Pray

Try to commit to at least eight minutes of prayer daily this week. Consider beginning with these prayer suggestions.

- **Week 5, Day 1:** Ask God to help you uncover doubts and to increase your faith.
- **Week 5, Day 2:** Thank God for the many convincing proofs that build your faith in Him.
- **Week 5, Day 3:** Promise God that you will do your part to increase your faith, reading and studying His word and praying daily.
- **Week 5, Day 4:** Ask God to help you to trust Him more and to pray faithfully.

Sing

"O for a Faith That Will Not Shrink," William Bathurst

Examine

In what circumstances do I tend to trust myself instead of God? Why is it that I turn inward in these situations instead of upward? What steps can I take today to begin trusting God more and myself less?

_____

_____

_____

_____

Discuss

Answer the following questions. Be ready to discuss them as a group.

1. One definition of _faith_ is "belief that does not rest on logical proof or material evidence." Is this definition accurate, inaccurate, or both? Explain. Can you think of a time when you heard someone suggest that biblical faith is unfounded or illogical? If so, be ready to share your experience(s). Why do you think people have this sort of understanding of faith?

_____

_____

_____

_____

2. The Bible says that God has given us "many convincing proofs" for our faith (Acts 1:3; see John 20:30–31). What convincing proofs cause you to trust God? Why? (Provide logical reasons and biblical examples.)

_____

_____

_____

_____

3. What kind of faith is described in Proverbs 3:5–7? How does this kind of faith affect our prayers? If we fail to develop this kind of faith, how might it affect our prayers?

_____

_____

_____

_____

God is Trustworthy

L ife is full of disappointments. Friends lie, spouses betray, employers cheat, leaders fail. The Bible echoes our experience, acknowledging that most people are unreliable: "Many a man proclaims his own loyalty, / But who can find a trustworthy man?" (Proverbs 20:6). There are plenty of reasons to become cynical and bitter. Yet in contrast to the faithlessness all around us, the Bible reveals that God is always faithful. He never lets us down. "For the Scripture says, 'Whoever

believes in Him will not be disappointed'" (Romans 10:11; see Isaiah 28:16; 1 Peter 2:6).

The faithfulness of God is at the heart of Christianity. Faithfulness means that God will never violate His own character, purpose, or word. He is fully consistent with Himself. The Bible says, "Know therefore that the LORD your God, He is God, the faithful God, who keeps His covenant and His lovingkindness to a thousandth generation with those who love Him and keep His commandments" (Deuteronomy 7:9; see 2 Timothy 2:13; 1 Corinthians 1:9). God is trustworthy. He never breaks a promise, He always acts like Himself, and He never slips out of character. He simply is and always will be God!

While it is easy to affirm that God is trustworthy, can we really *know* that He is? The answer is a resounding "Yes!" From the beginning, the Lord has shown Himself faithful. The psalmist said to God, "Your faithfulness continues throughout all generations" (Psalm 119:90), and of God, "all His work is done in faithfulness" (Psalm 33:4). The Lord has demonstrated His faithfulness in many ways:

- God created and preserves the universe (see Psalm 119:89–91; 33:4–9). The creative power and continued providence of God show Him to be "a faithful Creator" (1 Peter 4:19).
- God makes and fulfills wonderful promises to us (see Hebrews 10:23; 11.11). He has never made a promise that He has not kept.
- God protects us from evil and provides a way of escape (see 2 Thessalonians 3:3; 1 Corinthians 10:13). He wants us to succeed and comes alongside us to help. In other words, "The Lord knows how to rescue the godly from temptation" (2 Peter 2:9).

- God corrects us and forgives us when we fail (see Psalm 119:75; 1 John 1:9). The judgment of God is just (see Psalm 96:13). For those of us who are Christians, the Lord is a faithful friend who disciplines but also delivers (see Proverbs 27:6).
- God sanctifies us and prepares us for eternity (see 1 Thessalonians 5:23–24). He never gives up on us: "[He] will also confirm [us] to the end, blameless in the day of our Lord Jesus Christ. God is faithful" (1 Corinthians 1:8–9).

God always shows Himself trustworthy. The Bible, therefore, calls us to entrust ourselves to Him (see Hebrews 10:23).

One way we demonstrate our faith in God is through prayer. David prayed to God because he believed God was faithful to answer: "Hear my prayer, O LORD, / Give ear to my supplications! / Answer me in Your faithfulness, in Your righteousness!" (Psalm 143:1). Prayer is an act of faith. In prayer we acknowledge our inability to solve our problems or fix our failures (see Philippians 4:6–7; 1 John 1:8–9). When we trust the Lord, we will pray to Him.

One final example—Jeremiah. Everything in the prophet's life was falling apart. Jerusalem had been destroyed; Judah was in exile; the prophet was "alone." Yet in all these things, he could say, "This I recall to mind, / Therefore I have hope. / The LORD's lovingkindnesses indeed never cease, / For His compassions never fail. / They are new every morning; / Great is Your faithfulness" (Lamentations 3:21–23). God was faithful then, He is faithful now, and we can trust Him.

Pray

Try to commit to at least eight minutes of prayer daily this week. Consider beginning with these prayer suggestions.

- **Week 5, Day 5:** Thank God for His faithfulness, specifically for the ways in which He has demonstrated this to you personally.
- **Week 5, Day 6:** Promise God that you will respond to His faithfulness by being more faithful to Him.
- **Week 5, Day 7:** Confess to God any difficulties, anxieties, and sins you have been trying to solve on your own.

Sing

"Great Is Thy Faithfulness," Thomas Chisholm

Examine

What circumstances in my life tempt me to doubt the faithfulness of God? How have I responded to these circumstances in the past? What can I learn from these victories and failures that will help me to trust God more now?

_____

_____

_____

_____

Discuss

Answer the following questions. Be ready to discuss them as a group.

1. Read Proverbs 20:6. Why is it so hard to find faithful people? In what ways—both secular and religious—do people boast of their own loyalty or goodness? (see Luke 18:11–12) What do you think is meant by the word *trustworthy* in Proverbs 20:6?

_____

_____

_____

_____

2. In contrast to human faithlessness, God always shows Himself to be trustworthy. In what ways has God demonstrated that He is faithful? (Feel free to share both biblical and personal examples.) When you consider the faithfulness of God, what thoughts and emotions do you experience?

_____

_____

_____

_____

3. Read Psalm 143. David prayed because he trusted God. Since God always acts faithfully, righteously, and lovingly, for what did David pray? What did David remember in his prayer (v. 5)? What does Psalm 143 teach you about the faithfulness of God and the necessity of prayer?

_____

_____

_____

_____

The Essential Link Between Prayer and Bible Study

LESSON 11

When faith wanes, prayer suffers. God does not want this to happen, and neither should we. A weak faith is not a permanent predicament, however. When we trust in God, He helps us to grow. But the transition from mere intellectual acceptance of God to heartfelt trust in Him is not always easy. So how do we cultivate an authentic faith in God, a faith that results in greater devotion to Him and to prayer?

While there are likely several specific answers to this question, the Bible provides a simple yet profound starting point: "So faith comes from hearing, and hearing by the word of Christ" (Romans 10:17). Much of Romans focuses on faith, but there is another underlying theme—the power of God's word. Paul begins Romans with the following thesis: "I am not ashamed of the gospel, for it is the power of God for salvation to everyone who believes, to the Jew first and also to the Greek" (1:16). It isn't surprising, then, that the context of Romans 10:17 emphasizes the power of the word of God, showing us what the gospel is and what it can do in us.

- The word of God is not hurtful or depressing. It is good news about the good things that Jesus has done (v. 15). Though many do not accept it, the word of God has been faithfully delivered to us (v. 18).
- The word of God is not distant or vague. It is near to us, "in [our] mouth and in [our] heart" (v. 8), producing faith and prompting confession, resulting in our salvation (vv. 8–10). However, it is only when we hear the word that faith will come (vv. 14–17).

There is a necessary connection between the revelation of God and our faith. God discloses His word, and we respond in faith; but this process does not end at conversion. The Bible says, "Be diligent to present yourself approved to God as a workman who does not need to be ashamed, accurately handling the word of truth" (2 Timothy 2:15; see Acts 17:11). Without continued study, our faith deteriorates and our devotion to prayer does too. Faith simply cannot survive without constant exposure to the word of God (see Hebrews 5:11–12). There are no shortcuts. Since faith in God is vital to our relationship with Him, we must prioritize reading and meditating on His word. If we don't, our faith will eventually falter and fail.

Thanks be to God that He has given us His word in a way that we can understand and thus grow our faith! This is truly one of the great, spiritual blessings we have in Christ: "Blessed be the God and Father of our Lord Jesus Christ, who has blessed us with every spiritual blessing in the heavenly places in Christ…. In all wisdom and insight He made known to us the mystery of His will, according to the kind intention which He purposed in Him" (Ephesians 1:3, 8–9; see also 3:3–5). When we abide in the revealed word of God, our faith will grow.

But our relationship with God is more than *just* Bible study. A response is required. God wants us to speak to Him in prayer. Prayer and Bible study are thus interconnected: (1) God wants prayer to saturate our study of His word (see Psalm 119:18). (We will refer to this as "prayerful study.") (2) God also expects us to fill our prayers with biblical content (see Acts 4:25–26). (We will refer to this as "informed prayer.") Prayerful study and informed prayer have the potential to enliven and mobilize our faith, because they drive us back to God for more Bible study and prayer. The children's song got it right: "Read your Bible and pray every day, / And grow, grow, grow!"

If we long to grow in our faith and to be devoted to prayer, we must start by listening to God. This helps us to trust Him more, and, the more we trust God, the more we will pray to Him. It's that simple—and that challenging! So, let's set aside time today—and every day—to read our Bible and respond to God in faith and prayer.

Pray

Try to commit to at least nine minutes of prayer daily this week. Consider beginning with these prayer suggestions.

- **Week 6, Day 1:** Praise God for revealing His faith-producing word.
- **Week 6, Day 2:** Confess to God any weaknesses in your commitment to Bible study and prayer.
- **Week 6, Day 3:** Promise God that you will commit to daily interaction with Him through Bible study and prayer.
- **Week 6, Day 4:** Ask God to strengthen your resolve to listen and to speak to Him.

Sing

"Break Thou the Bread of Life," Mary Lathbury

Examine

Am I allowing God to speak to me daily through His written word? In my most recent Bible reading, what did I learn that increased my faith in God? If I am struggling, what is hindering me from devoting myself to Bible study, and what can I do to be more committed to it?

_____

_____

_____

_____

Discuss

Answer the following questions. Be ready to discuss them as a group.

1. Read Romans 10. How has God chosen to reveal His word to us? Why do you think God has revealed His word in this way? Explain the connection between God's word and our faith.

_____

_____

_____

_____

_____

_____

2. Read Hebrews 5:11–14. What is meant by the phrase *dull of hearing*? How can we become dull of hearing? What will happen if we fail to give adequate attention to Bible study? How can we avoid becoming dull of hearing?

_____

_____

_____

_____

3. Do you think that praying before, during, and/or after Bible study is important? Why, or why not? Do you think incorporating biblical words and phrases into our public and private prayers is helpful or harmful, or both? Why, or why not?

_____

_____

_____

_____

LESSON 12 — Prayer is "Risky"

When we pray, we are consciously entrusting ourselves to God, allowing His will (and not our own) to dictate the course of our lives. To unbelievers, this seems foolish—especially if we are facing distressing and even dangerous circumstances. Prayer is a "risk" that many people are simply unwilling to take.

What makes prayer seem so risky? Perhaps it is because prayer makes us vulnerable, and frankly, most of us are uncomfortable acknowledging our dependence on others and on God. If we are honest with ourselves, don't we "naturally" like to feel as if we are the masters of our own destiny? Prayer rubs against the grain of our egos and brings us face to face with the truth that there is little that we actually control. Prayer shows us that we need God and that only by trusting in Him will we find lasting peace.

There is a close connection between faith and prayer, and both involve some level of "risk." Faith is not risky because it lacks substance (Lesson 9). It is "risky," first, because it requires us to trust God when His methods and timing do not make sense to us and when personal loss is possible. This kind of faith was evident in Abraham: "By faith Abraham, when he was called, obeyed by going out to a place which he was to receive for an inheritance; and he went out, not knowing where he was going," and "By faith Abraham, when he was tested, offered up Isaac, and he who had received the promises was offering up his only begotten son" (Hebrews 11:8, 17). He trusted God even when the commands did not make sense. Second, prayer is "risky," because when we pray, we are acknowledging that God is in control, that we need Him, that He knows what He is doing, and that His timing is best. But, based on what we know about God (Part 1), the benefits of trusting God in prayer far outweigh any "losses" we may suffer.

Let's consider the example of Hezekiah in 2 Kings 18–20:

Hezekiah was king over Judah from 727 to 698 BC, a turbulent time in the history of the nation. Hezekiah's father Ahaz was a wicked ruler who had failed the nation but somehow produced a godly son. The Bible says Hezekiah was uniquely faithful to God. He was obedient, zealous, trusting, and committed (see 2 Kings 18:3–6). "He trusted in the LORD, the God of Israel.... He clung to the LORD.... And the LORD was with him" (2 Kings 18:5–7). What a biography!

There came a point for Hezekiah, however, when the rubber of his faith met the road of reality, and he had to decide whether he was going to "risk" putting everything in God's hands or try to solve his problems on his own. The Assyrians invaded Judah and came all the way to the gates of Jerusalem with this message: "Don't trust Hezekiah and his God. Surrender and live; or fight and die!" Hezekiah was greatly distressed, but at the brink of impending personal and national disaster, he did not abandon his faith. He trusted the promises of God and prayed (see 2 Kings 19:1–19). From a worldly perspective, Hezekiah took a big risk choosing faith and prayer, but it was, in reality, not risky at all. Why? Because God listened and acted, defeating the enemies of His people (see vv. 20–37).

The same God who heard Hezekiah listens to us (see Psalm 34:17). If we lay it all on the line, trusting that God will come through for us, we risk nothing of real consequence. We may lose our sense of self-security and our standing among the unbelieving elite—or even our lives!—but look at what we gain by putting ourselves fully in the hands of God—peace and protection (see Philippians 4:6–7).

Knowledge and faith take away the "riskiness" of prayer. Like Abraham and Hezekiah, prayer is worth the "risk." It works!

Pray

Try to commit to at least nine minutes of prayer daily this week. Consider beginning with these prayer suggestions.

- **Week 6, Day 5:** Confess to God any insecurity you feel and ask Him to help you be more confident in Him.
- **Week 6, Day 6:** Thank God for something specific that He did in your life after you handed a situation over to Him.
- **Week 6, Day 7:** Promise God that you will "risk" more for His sake, trusting that He will give you the strength that you need to persevere.

Sing

"Be Still My Soul," Katharina von Schlegel (Trans., Jane Borthwick)

Examine

Do I ever think that relying on prayer is too risky and try to solve my problems on my own? What can I learn about the importance of prayer from people in the Bible (e.g., Hezekiah)? What can I do today to implement the lessons that I learn from these people?

_____

_____

_____

_____

Discuss

Answer the following questions. Be ready to discuss them as a group.

1. Why might worldly people think prayer is foolish? If an unbeliever told you that you should not base your future on faith and prayer, how would you respond? Why might some Christians treat prayer as their last resort instead of their first response to the circumstances of life?

_____

_____

_____

_____

2. Read 2 Kings 19. What personal and national "risks" did Hezekiah take when he based the defense of his kingdom on faith and prayer? Did Hezekiah make a wise or foolish choice? Explain. What other Bible characters have acted like Hezekiah, trusting and praying to God for salvation?

_____

_____

_____

_____

3. What characteristics and promises of God make prayer seem less risky? Knowing these things, why do we sometimes continue to struggle with our commitment to prayer? What can we do to overcome our doubts and fears concerning faith and prayer?

_____

_____

_____

_____

Faith Changes Our Focus

A famous Greco-Roman myth describes an extraordinarily handsome man named Narcissus. When Narcissus was quite young, a prophet warned the child's parents that they should keep Narcissus from himself. For years, they did, but at sixteen years old, as Narcissus walked through a forest, a nymph named Echo saw him, fell madly in love with him, and followed him secretly. Recognizing that he was not alone, Narcissus called out, "Who's there?" to which Echo timidly repeated, "Who's there?" When Echo finally revealed her identity to Narcissus and attempted to embrace him, he stepped away and told her to leave him alone. Heartbroken, she spent the rest of her life in lonely valleys until nothing but hollow echoes remained of her. When Nemesis, the

goddess of vengeance, heard about this, she decided to punish Narcissus, luring him to a pool where he saw his own reflection for the first time. He became infatuated with himself, but when he recognized that his love could not be addressed, he committed suicide.

This ancient story describes the age-old vice of self-centeredness (or narcissism). Self-centeredness is a problem, because it always hurts oneself and others and, according to the Bible, offends God! "Egotism [or self-centeredness] is one of the repulsive manifestations of pride…. It leads one to consider everything in its relation to himself rather than in relation to God and the welfare of His people" (J. Oswald Sanders). From the very beginning, Satan has lured people into self-absorption and self-reliance, and the world has only gotten worse (see Genesis 3:5). Even today, many in our society are highly narcissistic, and we are not immune to the temptation to think of ourselves too highly (see Romans 12:3). If we allow ourselves to get caught up in selfishness, it will show up in every aspect of our lives—even in our prayers!

Before we go further, let's note that it is not selfish to make requests for ourselves to God. God tells us to do so (see 1 Peter 5:7; Philippians 4:6). However, there is a point when prayer stops being God-centered and becomes self-centered. How do we know when we have crossed the line?

Jesus told a parable—the Parable of the Pharisee and the Tax Collector—that helps us identify self-centered prayer (Luke 18:9–14). Our prayers may be self-centered if any of the descriptions of the Pharisee's prayer characterize our own: self-absorbed, self-promoting, disrespectful, condescending, and carnal (see vv. 11–12). How sad when prayer stops being an expression of faith and becomes a manifestation of pride! In contrast to the self-centered prayer of the Pharisee is the God-centered prayer of the tax collector. He prayed a simple, humble, reverent, penitent, and trusting prayer: "God, be merciful to me, the sinner!" (v. 13).

To avoid self-centered prayer, we must have faith. Faith keeps us from being selfish and prideful, because it forces us to acknowledge God. (How can we be egotistical in the shadow of an infinite God?!) The deeper our trust in God, the more we will seek His wisdom, His will, and His glory—and not our own. Perhaps one of the clearest examples of this kind of prayer is Jesus's Model Prayer in Matthew 6:9–13.

- The Model Prayer starts and ends with God (vv. 9, 13).
- The Model Prayer focuses more on God and less on self (vv. 9–10).
- The Model Prayer is more concerned with the spiritual providence of God than the physical (vv. 11–13).
- The Model Prayer evidences complete trust in God (vv. 9–13).

If we need help overcoming self-centeredness, the answer is not to stop praying but to pray differently. We need to pray like Jesus!

Faith changes the focus of our prayers, away from self and toward God. Prayer is less about us—though we do benefit from it. Prayer is more—or can we say, all—about God. Faith helps us to look away from ourselves and up to Him.

Pray

Try to commit to at least ten minutes of prayer daily this week. Consider beginning with these prayer suggestions.

- **Week 7, Day 1:** Ask God to help you identify and overcome any selfish tendencies with which you struggle.
- **Week 7, Day 2:** Promise God that you will fight selfishness and that you will be a God-centered person.
- **Week 7, Day 3:** Thank God for His patience with you and for His grace that makes you more like Jesus.
- **Week 7, Day 4:** Promise God that you will trust Him and pray God-focused prayers.

Sing

"None of Self and All of Thee," Theodore Monod

Examine

In what situations do I find myself being self-centered? As it relates to prayer, have I ever tried to use prayer as a tool to accomplish my own selfish purpose? What can I do to deepen my trust in God and make my prayers God-centered?

_____

_____

_____

_____

Discuss

Answer the following questions. Be ready to discuss them as a group.

1. List some people from the Bible who struggled with self-centeredness. What did these people say or do that manifested their selfishness? What do they teach us about self-centeredness and how to overcome it?

_____

_____

_____

_____

2. Read Luke 18:9–14. Why did Jesus tell the Parable of the Pharisee and the Tax Collector? What phrases in the Pharisee's prayer show that he was a self-centered person? Even though the tax collector was praying for himself, would you describe his prayer as self-centered? Why, or why not?

_____

_____

_____

_____

3. Read Matthew 6:5–13. The Model Prayer of Jesus is set in contrast to what kinds of prayers? Is the Model Prayer self-centered or God-centered? Explain. After studying the Model Prayer, what kinds of changes do we need to make in our private and public prayers?

_____

_____

_____

_____

How Do We Pray in Faith?

LESSON 14

Part 1: What It Doesn't Mean

Belief is essential to a devoted prayer life (Part 2). So what if we begin to question our faith? Not our fundamental faith in God but whether we really trust Him and know what to expect from Him? The Bible says, "But if any of you lacks wisdom, let him ask of God, who gives to all generously and without reproach, and it will be given to him. But he must ask in faith without any doubting, for the one who doubts is like the surf of the sea, driven and tossed by the wind" (James 1:5–6). We might ask ourselves, *Am I really praying in faith?* An honest answer to this question is important because the Bible continues, "For that man [who doubts] ought not to expect that he will receive anything from the Lord, being a double-minded man, unstable in all his ways" (vv. 7–8). The consequences of unbelief are frightening—ineffective prayer, purposeless existence, and widespread instability (see vv. 6–8).

The Lord desires something better for us. He wants us to know that we can come to Him in the worst of circumstances, ask Him for wisdom, and trust that He will be gracious (see vv. 2–5). The only way we can have this kind of relationship with God is by praying in faith. With many false notions about what praying in faith is, it is vital that we discern the truth on this subject. In our next study, we will explore *what it means* to pray in faith. In this study,

however, we will try to find out *what it doesn't mean.*

First, praying in faith does not mean that we simply pray optimistically. While it is important that we be cheerful and positive as Christians, the prayer of faith does not ignore problems and cite innocuous clichés. Rather, God expects us to bring Him the good and the bad—our hurts, our worries, our weaknesses (see James 1:2–5; Romans 8:26–27). The Bible says, "Therefore humble yourselves under the mighty hand of God, that He may exalt you at the proper time, casting all your anxiety on Him, because He cares for you" (1 Peter 5:6–7). Praying in faith is not just convincing ourselves that everything is good. If our prayers are that shallow, we will be disillusioned when bad things happen.

Next, praying in faith does not mean that we rely on our own spiritual ability. As noted in previous lessons, relying on ourselves always leads to disappointment and ruin (see Proverbs 14:12). Praying in faith means trusting in God (see 3:5–6). If, in our heart of hearts, we start to think that God will listen to us because of who we are and what we do—and not because of who He is—we are in grave danger. The Pharisee prayed, "I fast twice a week; I pay tithes of all that I get" (Luke 18:12). He trusted in himself, and Jesus described the Pharisee as "praying… to himself," not to God (v. 11). Prayers that rely on our own works end in pride (trusting ourselves) or frustration (blaming ourselves).

Finally, praying in faith does not mean that we always expect an affirmative answer. God always answers our prayers but not always with "Yes." He may say "No" or "Not yet." God is not a conciliatory grandfather who gives in to every request. As we noted in the first part of this workbook, God is omnipotent and omniscient; He knows what we need far better than we do. So if we think praying in faith means getting everything we want, we will be sorely disappointed.

In sum, praying in faith does not mean that we simply pray optimistically, that we rely on our own spiritual ability, or that we always get what we want.

In the next lesson, we will discuss what it really means to pray in faith. As a quick preview, praying in faith means trusting that God will give us the best answer to our requests.

Pray

Try to commit to at least ten minutes of prayer daily this week. Consider beginning with these prayer suggestions.

- **Week 7, Day 5:** Ask God to teach you what it means to pray in faith.
- **Week 7, Day 6:** Confess to God any erroneous ideas that you have had regarding what it means to pray in faith.
- **Week 7, Day 7:** Promise God that you will do your best to remove pride and self-centeredness from your prayers and trust Him more.

Sing

"My God, My Father, Though I Stray," Charlotte Elliott

Examine

Have I ever felt like my prayers were ineffective because I was not praying in faith? In those times, what did I think it meant to pray in faith? Was that view right or wrong? Based on what I know now, how have my prayers changed (or how do they need to change)?

_____

_____

_____

_____

Discuss

Answer the following questions. Be ready to discuss them as a group.

1. Read James 1:5–8. What does this passage tell us about God? What does it tell us about us? Are you encouraged or discouraged to pray after reading this passage? Explain.

_____

_____

_____

_____

2. It was suggested in this lesson that praying in faith does not mean that we merely pray optimistically, that we rely on our own spiritual ability, or that we always expect a positive answer. Do you agree or disagree? Explain, and provide scriptural support for your answer.

_____

_____

_____

_____

3. What other incorrect definitions of praying in faith have you heard or even held yourself? What kinds of disappointments come when we hold false ideas about what it means to pray in faith? If you were talking with a friend who was ready to give up on prayer because he or she felt like praying in faith was impossible for him or her, what would you say to help? (The next lesson will provide additional answers for the last question.)

_____

_____

_____

_____

LESSON 15 How Do We Pray in Faith?
Part 2: What It Does Mean

As we noted in our previous study, God desires that we pray in faith (see James 1:6). This does not mean that we merely pray optimistically, that we rely on our own spiritual ability, or that we always expect an affirmative answer from God. However, it is not enough simply to know what praying in faith is not; we must know what it is.

Not praying in faith results in several negative consequences: ineffective prayer, purposeless existence, and widespread instability (Lesson 14). Yet praying in faith brings great rewards: divine access and abundant blessings (see James 1:5; 5:15). Jesus Himself said, "Therefore I say to you, all things for which you pray and ask, believe that you have received them, and they will be granted to you" (Mark 11:24). Don't we all want that kind of assurance? If so, we must pray in faith. But how do we do so?

We start by identifying the object of our faith—God. Praying in faith does not necessarily mean that we need to pray some special class of prayers but that we pray from the right perspective—focused on the person and character of God (Part 1). If we are going to pray like this, we need continued, authentic interaction with the Lord, seeing Him as He is and honoring all that He does and expects of us (see Mark 11:24; 14:26).

Our personal, subjective faith plays an important part in the quality of our prayers. Yet Christ is the one who makes possible our confident access to God. Regardless of our feelings at any given time, the Lord assures us that we can always approach Him in prayer, that He never ignores us, and that He wants to grant our requests (see Hebrews 4:16; 1 John 5:13–14; Matthew 7:7–11). Praying in faith means we know God is listening to our prayers and is actively working all things together for good (see Romans 8:28). This does not mean everything in this life will be good! But we can trust that however God answers our requests (e.g., "Yes," "No," "Not yet") He has our ultimate, eternal good in mind. We can trust that He knows what is best for us (Ephesians 3:20).

Praying in faith begins with a focused faith, but it does not end there. It also involves at least two additional components: persistence and submission.

Persistence. Faith and persistent prayer are closely connected in Scripture. In Luke 18, Jesus spoke about a widow who was continually approaching an unrighteous judge asking for legal protection. Though the judge did not care about the woman's plight, he granted her request because she kept asking him (vv. 2–5). Similarly, God listens to us when we pray to Him, but unlike the judge, God enjoys hearing from us (vv. 6–8). So if we want to pray in faith, we must learn the lesson of the parable: "at all times [we] ought to pray and not to lose heart" (v. 1).

Submission. But what if we keep on praying and God does not grant our request? The next part of praying in faith is that we submit to God. For example, while Paul trusted God and persisted in prayer, his specific request in 2 Corinthians 12 was not granted. Instead, God gave Him something better—grace! Paul responded, "Most gladly, therefore, I will rather boast about my weaknesses, so that the power of Christ may dwell in me" (2 Corinthians 12:9; see vv. 7–10). That is the kind of submission we need if we too want to pray in faith. We must accept when God says "Yes" and when He says "No."

There are no magic formulas. Praying in faith simply means that we know and trust God, that we actively and persistently pray to Him, and that we accept His answers. When our faith and prayer meet, we will begin to see with clarity through the fog of our present reality into the bliss of the spiritual realm. Then our prayers will accomplish much and bring God great pleasure (see James 5:15–16; Hebrews 13:15–16).

Pray

Try to commit to at least eleven minutes of prayer daily this week. Consider beginning with these prayer suggestions.

- **Week 8, Day 1:** Ask God to help you to know Him as He is so that you can pray in faith.
- **Week 8, Day 2:** Promise God that you will pray to Him persistently.
- **Week 8, Day 3:** Confess to God any failures in submission and promise to accept His answers to your prayers.
- **Week 8, Day 4:** Thank God that His grace is sufficient for you.

Sing

"'Tis the Blessed Hour of Prayer," Fanny Crosby

Examine

Do I ever feel like the quality of my faith hinders my prayers from reaching God? If so, is the problem with my knowledge of the object of my faith (God), with my persistence, with my attitude, with a combination of these issues, or with something else altogether? What can I do to overcome this hindrance(s) and pray in faith?

_____

_____

_____

_____

Discuss

Answer the following questions. Be ready to discuss them as a group.

1. Read Mark 11:12–14, 20–26. Jesus wants His disciples to pray in faith. What attitudes and actions prevent this? What commands does Jesus give for overcoming these issues? Compare Mark 11:20–26 with 1 John 5:13–15. Are these passages promising that we will receive every request we make of God? Explain.

_____

_____

_____

_____

_____

_____

2. Read Luke 18:1–8. Why did Jesus tell the Parable of the Widow and the Unrighteous Judge? What does this parable teach us about God and prayer? The parable focuses on prayer, but at the end, Jesus asks whether He will find what on the earth at His coming? What does this tell us about the connection between prayer and faith?

_____

_____

_____

3. Read 2 Corinthians 12:7–10. Do you think there was a problem with the faith (or the prayers) of Paul that kept God from granting His request? Why, or why not? By saying that His grace was sufficient, was God in any way shortchanging Paul? Why, or why not? Does this passage encourage or discourage you from praying? Explain.

_____

_____

_____

_____

LESSON 16 Prayer Proves Our Faith

In Part 2 ("Believe") we have noted how faith in God affects our prayers. Our devotion to prayer will be firmly established and strengthened when our faith takes on the characteristics that we have studied. In this final lesson of the second section, we will adjust our viewpoint slightly and examine prayer as the proof (or authentication) of our faith.

As we saw in the last lesson, Jesus connects persistent prayer with authentic faith (see Luke 18:1–8). He was probably encouraging His disciples to pray in view of the coming judgment against Jerusalem (see Luke 17:22–37). With this ominous event looming on the horizon, the saints needed to be resolute and relentless in their prayers. He concluded: "When the Son of Man comes, will He find faith on the earth?" (Luke 18:8). Though the circumstances are not identical, isn't this question relevant to us as well in view of the final coming of Christ? The context of Luke 18 points us to this truth: for Jesus to find faith at the end, we must be praying fervently until the end. Prayer is, therefore, one of the primary indicators of our faith.

The Bible teaches us that it is possible to determine whether faith is real or not (see James 2:18). If the external manifestations of our faith are not present, then something is wrong with the internal quality of our faith. Jesus said, "The good man brings out of his good treasure what is good; and the evil man bring out of his evil treasure what is evil" (Matthew 12:35). If

we are not doing the good work of prayer, we need to take an honest look at ourselves and examine our faith (see 2 Corinthians 13:5).

Lest we become discouraged and doubt our faith altogether, let's remember that prayer is a spiritual discipline that must be developed (Lesson 17). In fact, the desire to pray more zealously and consistently demonstrates that our faith is not dead but is alive and quite possibly on the verge of its next great cycle of growth.

So how does prayer prove our faith? If we are praying—not just going through the motions at mealtimes and bedtime but really, continually, and fervently praying—it manifests a heartfelt trust in God. It shows that we really believe prayer works and that it is not merely some empty, religious ritual (see Mark 11:24; James 5:16). Are we still working to get to that level of dedication to prayer? Let's not give up! There will be ups and downs, but if we keep watch on our prayer life, we will have a good idea when we need to work on our faith.

Our commitment to prayer is not just an indicator of the quality of our faith. It also

develops it. We've already noted that the means of growing faith is the word of God (Lesson 11). Yet, prayer, being our response to God and His revelation, exercises and matures our faith. Like physical fitness, faith requires not only that we adequately feed ourselves on the Bible but also that we use our spiritual muscles and exercise our faith in God, praying to Him and doing other good works (see 1 Timothy 4:6–8). Like the apostles, we need to "devote ourselves to prayer and to the ministry of the word," because both are needed (Acts 6:4).

Prayer is an essential facet of our relationship with God. It proves and develops our faith. We simply cannot "do" faith without it.

With these things in mind, we can now move to Part 3. But let's not forget the first two sections as we discuss the practical and personal elements of prayer. Knowing and trusting God are the foundations. Ideally, these concepts have already changed some aspects of our prayer life. Part 3 is intended to further develop our understanding of prayer itself and to motivate us to action.

Pray

Try to commit to at least eleven minutes of prayer daily this week. Consider beginning with these prayer suggestions.

- **Week 8, Day 5:** Praise God that faith and prayer are interconnected and available to us.
- **Week 8, Day 6:** Promise God that you will habitually evaluate the quality of your prayers, recognizing that this demonstrates the quality of your faith.
- **Week 8, Day 7:** Thank God for the spiritual benefits that come from prayer, specifically that it develops and enlivens our faith.

Sing

"Take Time to Be Holy," William Longstaff

Examine

Does the quality of my prayer life demonstrate that I possess a strong, vibrant faith? If so, what bold request should I make and act on today to bring glory to God? If not, what aspects of my faith and prayer life do I need to work on to get back on track?

_____

_____

_____

_____

Discuss

Answer the following questions. Be ready to discuss them as a group.

1. Read Matthew 12:33–37. What other passages show that our actions reveal our heart? Do you think it is true that our commitment to prayer reveals the quality of our faith? Why, or why not?

_____

_____

_____

_____

2. Why is it sometimes difficult for us to evaluate our own spiritual condition? Think of a time(s) when your commitment to prayer was weak. What convicted you of your failure(s)? If it was a specific Bible passage(s), be ready to share it with the class.

_____

_____

_____

_____

3. Do you agree that prayer is a spiritual exercise that develops our faith? Why, or why not? What connection(s) is there between Bible study, prayer, and faith? Do you tend to study more or pray more? What do you feel is a healthy ratio of time spent in Bible study/meditation and time spent in prayer?

_____

_____

_____

_____

PART 3

ENGAGE

PART 3

ENGAGE

LESSON 17 Prayer Requires Discipline

In nearly every world religion, there are practices that are referred to, in one way or another, as "spiritual disciplines." While the word *discipline* itself has a variety of meanings, we will define *spiritual disciplines* as "exercises (behaviors) that train us toward greater spirituality." It should not surprise us that most—if not all—religions include prayer in their list of disciplines. The discipline of prayer truly develops our spirituality (Lesson 16).

Like all spiritual disciplines, prayer requires another kind of discipline—self-discipline. Jesus Himself, on various occasions, taught the need for persistence in prayer, no doubt, anticipating our failure to discipline ourselves to pray as consistently as we should (see Luke 11:5–10; 18:1–8). The apostle Paul, likewise, wrote that we should "pray without ceasing" and "devote [ourselves] to prayer, keeping alert in it with an attitude of thanksgiving" (1 Thessalonians 5:17; Colossians 4:2). We cannot obey these commands without discipline.

Perhaps the most explicit connection between discipline and prayer is made by Peter. He says, "The end of all things is near; therefore, be of sound judgment and sober spirit for the purpose of prayer" (1 Peter 4:7). We learn from this passage what is needed to discipline ourselves in prayer: a proper perspective concerning the future and concerning the present.

First, we need a proper perspective concerning the future. Peter says plainly that "the end of all things is near." While there is debate regarding the proper identification of "the end of all things," it is possible to interpret this as the literal ending of all things (see Romans 13:11–12). If this is correct, the phrase "is near" must be taken in a relative sense, that all things have been accomplished and the end could come at any moment. If this became our view of the future, wouldn't it result in greater devotion to prayer? Peter seemed to think so.

Second, we need a proper perspective concerning the present. Peter draws the conclusion that our view of the future will affect our view of the present (see 2 Peter 3:11–12). He says, "Therefore, be of sound judgment and sober spirit." The first word, which is translated "be of sound judgment," is an obvious reference to our need to exercise self-control, and the second, "be of sober spirit," reinforces the idea. We cannot get distracted. We are temporary residents in hostile territory, engaged in a battle for our souls (see 1 Peter 2:11). We fight formidable enemies, and without self-discipline and prayer, the battle is lost (see Ephesians 6:10–18).

What does this look like in real life? The specific applications will differ from person to person, but here are some common elements:

- Moral Discipline. We need to be morally disciplined (see 1 Corinthians 9:24–27). If the purpose of self-discipline is effective prayer, the result of self-indulgence is ineffective prayer (see Proverbs 15:8; 1 Peter 3:7). If we are unwilling to turn away from sin, it is unlikely that we will be devoted to prayer.
- Mental Discipline. We also need to be mentally disciplined (see Hebrews 12:1–3). There are so many "innocent" thoughts and activities that can steal our time, energy, and focus. We therefore need desperately to exercise self-control and to prioritize prayer.

The intended result of transforming our perspective of the future and of the present and disciplining ourselves is revealed in 1 Peter 4:7: "for the purpose of prayer." When we discipline ourselves, Peter says we will pray frequently and persistently. Surely that is our desire as Christians, but it starts and ends with discipline.

Let's decide to be more disciplined today (and in the future) than we have been in the past. The result will be greater devotion to the discipline of prayer, resulting in greater spirituality and preparing us for eternity.

Pray

Try to commit to at least twelve minutes of prayer daily this week. Consider beginning with these prayer suggestions.

- **Week 9, Day 1:** Confess to God ways you have failed to discipline yourself, specifically in prayer.
- **Week 9, Day 2:** Promise God that you will give more thought to the final judgment and that you will pray accordingly.
- **Week 9, Day 3:** Ask God to give you strength to be morally and mentally disciplined.
- **Week 9, Day 4:** Praise God for the transformation that He has already worked in you, and promise Him that you will allow Him to continue to change you in the future.

Sing

"Yield Not to Temptation," Horatio Palmer

Examine

Do I spend enough time considering that the end of all things is near and that I am in the midst of a spiritual struggle with wicked forces? How can I become (more) morally and mentally disciplined? If I am presently trying to discipline myself, what is my purpose? Is it for prayer and God's glory, or for other reasons?

_____

_____

_____

Discuss

Answer the following questions. Be ready to discuss them as a group.

1. Why is it so difficult to discipline ourselves? Do you believe that discipline is a vital part of devotion to prayer? Why, or why not? How can we become (more) disciplined people? Think of several ways. Do not confine yourself to the lesson or the passages listed in it.

_____

_____

_____

_____

2. Read 1 Peter 4:1–19. (If possible, read all of 1 Peter.) Discuss the possible interpretations of the statement "the end of all things is near" (v. 7). Based on each of these interpretations, why would Peter encourage sound judgment and sobriety? Does this encourage you to greater commitment to prayer? Explain.

_____

_____

_____

3. Why is it important that we discipline ourselves morally and mentally? Which challenge— moral or mental discipline—do you feel hinders more Christians from being fully devoted to prayer? Explain.

_____

_____

_____

_____

LESSON 18 We Must Dedicate Time to Prayer

Steve Jobs is credited as saying, "My favorite things in life don't cost any money. It's really clear that the most precious resource we all have is time." If people of the world perceive the value of time, how much more should we (Christians) recognize and capitalize spiritually on the opportunities we are given! The Bible says, "Therefore be careful how you walk, not as unwise men but as wise, making the most of your time, because the days are evil" (Ephesians 5:15–16).

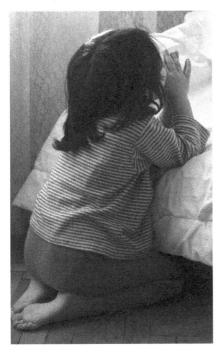

How should we be spending our time? The Bible does not specify a daily schedule; it simply tells us to use our time wisely and spiritually (see Ephesians 5:15–16; Romans 12:1–2). This does not mean that our time must be spent only in Bible study, meditation, and prayer, or that we are mismanaging our time if we involve ourselves in vocational, social, or recreational activities. Even spiritual people, like Jesus, spent time in "non-spiritual" activities (see Mark 6:3, 31; John 2:2). However, an ever-present danger is that we can—and often do—saturate our schedules with the latter to the neglect of the former. It is important that we schedule and prioritize spiritual activities.

We need to set aside time for prayer. This is not to say that we are limited to praying only at scheduled times. We can and should pray spontaneously throughout the day. However, it is important that we specifically designate time for prayer. The Old and New Testaments emphasize the value of habitual prayer:

- David started each day with prayer (Psalm 5:3).
- Daniel prayed three times daily (Daniel 6:10).
- Jesus regularly spent time alone in prayer, even though His schedule was full (Luke 5:16; Mark 6:31).
- The apostles delegated certain spiritual activities to others so that they could devote themselves to prayer (Acts 6:4).

Daily prayer was obviously important to these spiritual men. Is it just as important to us?

While most of us acknowledge the need for daily prayer, we may still struggle with beginning and maintaining the habit. Perhaps the following suggestions will help.

First, it is vital that we choose a specific time and place for prayer. Each of us probably has a certain time (e.g., morning, afternoon, nighttime) and place (e.g., bedroom, backyard, commute) when and where we pray with greater clarity and intensity (see Appendix 1). It helps to schedule our prayer time for that time and place. Yet even if we are unable to pray at our prime time, we should still assign time for prayer or it will probably not happen. It may be helpful to schedule Bible study and prayer together into what is popularly called a "devotional" or "quiet time."

Second, it is important that we employ a personally engaging, biblical method of prayer. We may need to explore different positions and procedures to identify those that aid our approach to God (e.g., praying audibly, silently, or in written form; eyes open or closed; head and hands lowered or raised; see Appendix 1).

Third, it is essential that we commit to a daily prayer schedule for an extended period of time. Habits are rarely established after a single day of activity. If we want to keep a daily time of prayer, we need to persevere for several weeks. We may not do so perfectly at first, but if we continue after failure, we are more likely to succeed. (More on this in Lesson 24.)

Fourth, it is good to establish some level of accountability. While we can commit to prayer alone, it is much easier with the help of other Christians who also pray regularly. Texting, email, and social media are great ways to ask one another for help in prayer.

Time is precious. God wants us to make the most of it. One worthy use of our time is prayer. Let's start (and continue) a prayer habit today!

Pray

Try to commit to at least twelve minutes of prayer daily this week. Consider beginning with these prayer suggestions.

- **Week 9, Day 5:** Thank God that He has given you time to live and pray. Confess any misuse of your time today.
- **Week 9, Day 6:** Ask God to help you develop a prayer habit like that of the spiritual men and women of the Bible.
- **Week 9, Day 7:** Promise God that you will allocate time to prayer, rehearsing what steps you will take to begin and maintain the habit.

Sing

"**I Will Pray,**" Annie Cummings

Examine

Have I, for the most part, used my time wisely and spiritually today? In what way(s) have I misused my time? How much time have I spent in prayer today? What can I do to ensure that I allot sufficient time to prayer (and other spiritual endeavors) daily?

_____

_____

_____

_____

Discuss

Answer the following questions. Be ready to discuss them as a group.

1. David, Daniel, Jesus, and the apostles are examples of people who prioritized daily prayer. Why do you think prayer was so important to them? What sacrifices did these men make to pray regularly? What might we need to sacrifice to be like them? (Optional Question: Who are other men and women in the Bible who made prayer a priority?)

_____

_____

_____

_____

2. Read Acts 6:1–6. Was it right for the apostles to forsake an important ministry for the sake of prayer? Why, or why not? What activities—good or bad—may we have to change or give up to have enough time for prayer (and Bible study)?

_____

_____

_____

_____

3. "To begin and maintain a daily time of prayer we need to choose a specific time and place, employ a personally engaging, biblical method of prayer, commit for an extended period of time, and establish some level of accountability." Do you agree or disagree with this statement? Explain. What modifications or additions would you make to these suggestions?

_____

_____

_____

_____

LESSON 19

The Kinds of Prayers God Rewards

In the Sermon on the Mount, Jesus counseled his disciples, "Beware of practicing your righteousness before me to be noticed by them; otherwise you have no reward with your Father who is in heaven" (Matthew 6:1). He illustrated this principle with several righteous acts—charity, prayer, and fasting (vv. 2–18). Regardless of the deed, the contrast is always the same: those who act to be seen by people have their reward in full (vv. 2, 5, 16). Those who work secretly will be blessed by God (vv. 4, 6, 18). From this, we learn that God rewards some prayers and rejects others.

So what kinds of prayers does God reward?

First, God rewards *authentic* prayers. Jesus says, "When you pray, you are not to be like the hypocrites; for they love to stand and pray in the synagogues and on the street corners so that they may be seen by men. Truly I say to you, they have their reward in full. But you, when you pray, go in your inner room, close your door and pray to your Father who is in secret, and your Father who sees what is done in secret will reward you" (Matthew 6:5–6). The intent of hypocritical prayers is to draw the attention of people, not God (see John 12:43). Though hypocrites receive temporary praise, they miss the eternal rewards that come from God. Authentic prayers are God-centered and are typically personal and private. When our prayers are free of false motives, God promises to listen and answer (see James 4:3, 10).

Second, God rewards *thoughtful* prayers. Jesus continues, "And when you are praying, do not use meaningless repetition as the Gentiles do, for they suppose that they will be heard for their many words. So do not be like them; for your Father knows what you need before you ask Him" (Matthew 6:7–8). The pagans, having abandoned the knowledge of God, tried to manipulate their deities. They repeated the same words or sentiments over and over again to inform the spiritual realm of human affairs and to convince their gods to listen (see 1 Kings 18:25–29). Jesus does not want us to be like the heathen. He wants us to know that God is paternal, omniscient, and accessible. When we come to know God, we will not offer hollow truisms but will thoughtfully approach Him.

Sadly, some religious people have ignored this command and have turned prayer into an empty ritual, rehearsing the same thoughts and words every time they pray. Ironically, even though the Model Prayer of Jesus in Matthew 6:9–13 immediately follows the prohibition against meaningless repetition, some only pray this prayer to God. (We will discuss the importance of variety in our prayers in Lessons 20 and 21.) Jesus is not condemning persistence in prayer, but he is forbidding vain repetition (see Luke 18:1–8; Hebrews 11:6). God rewards thoughtful prayers.

Third, God rewards *humble* yet *confident* prayers. While the descriptions humble and confident may appear contradictory, Jesus assumes both in His Model Prayer (see Matthew 6:9–13). Concerning the importance of humility, that Jesus must teach us to pray shows that even our knowledge of prayer is dependent on Him (see Luke 11:1–2; 1 Corinthians 4:6–7). Moreover, since the Model Prayer exalts and praises God, we know that prayer should not be focused on the one who is praying but on the Lord. It is God who provides, pardons, and protects (see Matthew 6:9–13; Lesson 22).

Humility does not, however, imply uncertainty. Jesus shows that we can boldly come to God. He is our Father (see Romans 8:15; Galatians 4:6). He hears and answers His children (see Matthew 7:7–11; 1 John 5:14–15). We can, therefore, approach Him with confidence—so long as we are living blamelessly and graciously (see Matthew 6:12–15; 5:23–24; 1 Peter 3:7). When humility and assurance intersect in prayer, God listens and blesses.

To sum up, God rewards authentic, thoughtful, humble, and confident prayers. He provides us with access to Him, guidance, providence, forgiveness, security, and much more. These rewards (treasures) are eternal (see Matthew 6:19–21). Prayer is indeed a worthy investment.

Pray

Try to commit to at least thirteen minutes of prayer daily this week. Consider beginning with these prayer suggestions.

- **Week 10, Day 1:** Thank God for His teaching concerning prayer.
- **Week 10, Day 2:** Promise God that you will pray authentically, thoughtfully, humbly, and confidently in the future.
- **Week 10, Day 3:** Confess to God any hypocritical, mindless, or prideful prayers that you have prayed recently.
- **Week 10, Day 4:** Ask God to embolden you to approach Him as He desires.

Sing

"Come, My Soul, Your Plea Prepare," John Newton (Arr., Craig Roberts)

Examine

Have I ever fallen into a habit of mindlessly praying the same prayer (or same kind of prayer)? In those times, did I feel engaged in the prayer that I was offering to God? If this is not currently a problem, what has helped me overcome this problem in the past?

_____

_____

_____

_____

Discuss

Answer the following questions. Be ready to discuss them as a group.

1. Read Matthew 6:5–13. What kinds of prayers does Jesus condemn, and why? What kinds of prayers does God reward, and why?

_____

_____

_____

_____

2. Do you tend to struggle more with praying like the hypocrites or like the heathen? Why? What helps you overcome the temptation to pray like the hypocrites and like the heathen? Explain.

_____

_____

_____

_____

3. What helps you to stay humble when you pray? Who are some biblical examples of people who prayed humbly? What does it mean and what does it not mean to pray boldly? Why are we sometimes hesitant to pray boldly? What are some biblical examples of people who prayed boldly? What can we learn from them?

_____

_____

_____

_____

LESSON 20 Praying Different Kinds of Prayers
Part 1

God loves diversity and creativity. He Himself is unique and imaginative. The Bible says, "O LORD, how many are Your works! / In wisdom You have made them all; / The earth is full of Your possessions" (Psalm 104:24). The many works of God evidence intricate design and careful precision and show our Creator's wisdom, power, and appreciation of beauty (see Psalm 104).

God has also uniquely crafted people. He gives each of us a distinct personality and skill set (see Romans 12:4–8; 1 Corinthians 12:4–11). He expects us to bring that uniqueness to Him in worship and service, even in our prayers (see Romans 12:1; Ephesians 2:10). God does not desire vain repetition (Lesson 19). He recognizes our diverse temperaments, vocabularies, and circumstances and expects us to approach Him as we are.

We know that God accepts different expressions of prayer because the prayers recorded in the Bible are themselves varied. The prayers of Moses differ from Hannah's. Those of Nehemiah are not identical to Paul's. There is also great variety among the psalmists. All these prayed different prayers in different ways yet they called on the same Lord. In the same way, our prayers will look different from others' because our circumstances, motivations, and purposes are varied, but we are bringing our diversity to the same God.

Not only do we pray differently from others, often we do not even pray the same prayers personally. In the documented prayers of Jesus, there are changes in content and style. When He was teaching His disciples to pray, He taught them the Model Prayer (Matthew 6:9–13). Just before the so-called Great Invitation, He offered a prayer of praise to God for His mysterious yet perfect plan (Matthew 11:25–26). Jesus later prayed an explicit, passionate request for deliverance: "My Father, if it is possible, let this cup pass from Me; yet not as I will but as You will" (Matthew 26:39; see v. 42). Jesus did not pray the same prayer every time; His prayers matched the situation and sentiment; and so must ours—even if that results in changes from prayer to prayer.

We should learn to pray with variety for several reasons: God commands it, life demands it, and blessings come from it.

First, we should pray with variety, because *God commands it.* The Bible says, "First of all, then, I urge that entreaties and prayers, petitions and thanksgivings, be made on behalf of all men" (1 Timothy 2:1). The word *urge* may be slightly less direct than other words (e.g., *demand, require*) but it still carries the force of a command. Therefore, God expects us to pray different prayers (entreaties, prayers, petitions, thanksgivings) for all people. (These different kinds of prayers will be defined in the next lesson.)

Second, we should pray with variety, because *life demands it.* As noted earlier, our circumstances are rarely identical from one prayer to the next. The intention and content of our prayers must, therefore, change too. We pray according to the need of the moment. We may praise God in one prayer but petition Him in the next, or make a personal request now and intercede for others later.

Third, we should pray with variety, because *blessings come from it.* The first blessing associated with praying different kinds of prayers is the simple joy of expanding our communication (and relationship) with God. Yet prayer also provides protection against self-centeredness, allowing us to rely on God and others, instead of ourselves (see Philippians 2:3–5).

Praying different kinds of prayers works; this is not to say that we must mechanically say just the right kind of prayer to get through to God; but when we approach God appropriately, He hears and acts (see Romans 8:26–27; 1 John 5:14–15). Prayer works, and God uses prayer to work in us and for us.

Why should we pray different kinds of prayers? Because God expects it and we need it. In our next study, we will discover the different kinds of prayers that we can offer to God.

Pray

Try to commit to at least thirteen minutes of prayer daily this week. Consider beginning with these prayer suggestions.

- **Week 10, Day 5:** Praise God for His creativity as manifested in his creation.
- **Week 10, Day 6:** Promise God that you will try your best to be yourself when you communicate with Him in the future.
- **Week 10, Day 7:** Thank God for the blessings associated with praying different kinds of prayers.

Sing

"Sweet Hour of Prayer," William Walford

Examine

How often do I consider the complex, creative nature of God? When I do, how does it affect my prayers? What unique qualities has God given me that I can use to add diversity to my prayers?

_____

_____

_____

_____

Discuss

Answer the following questions. Be ready to discuss them as a group.

1. Why do some people mindlessly repeat the same words, phrases, or sentiments in their prayers? Is this effective and pleasing to God? Why, or why not? Do you feel that it is good or bad to pray with variety? Explain.

_____

_____

_____

_____

2. Why should we learn to pray different kinds of prayers? (Do not confine yourself to the reasons given in the lesson.) Which of these reasons most motivates you to pray with variety? Why?

_____

_____

_____

_____

3. While our private and public prayers will necessarily differ from one another, it is easy to fall into the trap of using the same words and phrases when we pray as a group. Should we pray with variety in our public prayers? Why, or why not? What can we do to avoid mindless repetition in public prayers? If you do not lead public prayers, how can you encourage prayer leaders to pray with variety?

_____

_____

_____

_____

LESSON 21 Praying Different Kinds of Prayers
Part 2

In our last study, we noted the value of different kinds of prayers and identified several reasons why it is good to pray with variety. While it is important that we know why we should pray different kinds of prayers, we cannot stop there; we also need to know what kinds of prayers we can and should offer to God.

In 1 Timothy 2:1, several descriptions of prayer are identified. The passage says, "First of all, then, I urge that entreaties and prayers, petitions and thanksgivings, be made on behalf of all men." Let's consider each of these kinds of prayers:

- Entreaties. Entreaties (or supplications) are prayers in which we bring personal needs to God, asking Him to intervene on our behalf. God does not limit the nature or number of requests that we can make; He allows us to bring any and all of our concerns to Him (see 1 Peter 5:7).
- Prayers. Prayers are like entreaties in many respects, but the word translated "prayers" seems to be slightly more generic and includes various categories. This demonstrates that we can include multiple kinds of prayers within a single prayer. The word *prayer* implies a deep personal devotion to God, which should actually be the aim of all communication with God.
- Petitions. The word translated "petitions" is rare in the New Testament. Its meaning is somewhat difficult to determine. The intent seems to be that of confident access to God wherein we can bring petitions, either positive (intercessions) or negative (imprecations). In light of New Testament teaching and the immediate context of 1 Timothy 2:1, it seems that we should be making positive petitions on behalf of others (see Matthew 5:44).
- Thanksgivings. Thanksgivings are prayers that express feelings of gratitude to God. More than the other descriptions of prayer, thanksgivings are especially focused on God, praising Him for His goodness—though our thanks can be for others as well.

These descriptions illustrate the variety that God allows and expects in our prayers. We should strive to incorporate these concepts into our communication with God.

A word of warning, however. While it is good for us to understand the words in 1 Timothy 2:1, prayer must never become merely an intellectual exercise (Lesson 8). If, for example, we begin to think "I will learn to say a prayer of petition just so and God will do such-and-such," we will eventually be disappointed. We should not focus on the definitions to the exclusion of praying what needs to be prayed. We ought to engage the mind and the heart (see John 4:23–24).

If, however, we find ourselves praying the same prayer (or the same kind of prayer) all the time, we probably need to give more thought to the different kinds of prayers described in the Bible, move out of our comfort zone, and pray differently. We may need to reevaluate the way we are praying and employ positions and methods better suited to the immediate situation. For instance, while bowing our heads and closing our eyes is appropriate, this is not the only position for prayer. In the Bible, people prayed in various postures: bowing, sitting, kneeling, and even prostrating themselves (see Exodus 34:8; 1 Chronicles 17:16; 1 Kings 8:54; Ezra 10:1). To these we could add several other ideas: eyes up or down, open or shut; hands raised or lowered, open or clasped; audible, silent, or written prayers. In all the biblical examples, the position and method in some way reflected the sentiment of the prayer. The same must be true of ours. It can be difficult to change habits, especially if we have been praying the same way for a long time; but when we see commands and examples in the Bible that challenge or complement what we are doing, we should be willing to try something new.

God expects us to pray different kinds of prayers. This is not an obligation. It is a privilege. May the Lord bless us as we pray different, suitable, God-honoring prayers.

Pray

Try to commit to at least fourteen minutes of prayer daily this week. Consider beginning with these prayer suggestions.

- **Week 11, Day 1:** Ask God to teach you how to pray different kinds of prayers and to use appropriate positions and methods.
- **Week 11, Day 2:** Thank God that He allows you to approach Him in various ways.
- **Week 11, Day 3:** Confess to God any false ideas you have had concerning prayer or any times you have ritualized prayer.
- **Week 11, Day 4:** Promise God that you will continue to learn and employ different kinds of prayers.

Sing

"Hear Now Our Prayers," Claude Worley

Examine

Do I pray the various kinds of prayers listed in 1 Timothy 2:1 (entreaties, prayers, petitions, thanksgivings)? Do I overemphasize a certain kind of prayer to the neglect of others? If so, what kind, and what can I do to balance my prayers?

_____

_____

_____

_____

Discuss

Answer the following questions. Be ready to discuss them as a group.

1. Read 1 Timothy 2:1–8. What different kinds of prayers are listed? In your own words, describe each of these prayers. Who benefits when we pray different kinds of prayers? In what way(s)? Regardless of the specific type of prayer, what should characterize our prayers?

_____

_____

_____

_____

2. What are the benefits of defining and analyzing the various descriptions of prayer? What are some of the dangers? How can we ensure that we benefit from a greater knowledge of the different types of prayer that God allows us to pray?

_____

_____

_____

_____

3. In the lesson, it was suggested that we may need to force ourselves to pray different kinds of prayers and change our position(s) and method(s) of prayer. Do you agree or disagree? Explain. Why do you think many Christians employ the same manner of prayer—eyes closed, head bowed, hands clasped—every time they pray?

_____

_____

_____

_____

LESSON 22
How Can We Pray More Passionately?

How sad when prayer becomes simply an exercise of the mind, devoid of emotion and divorced from reality! God intends prayer to be much more—a demonstration of authenticity, trust, and emotion. If our interaction with God is mindless and impersonal, we need to seriously evaluate our spiritual condition and make necessary adjustments (see Isaiah 29:13). Then our prayers can be passionate.

The Bible says, "Now I urge you, brethren, by our Lord Jesus Christ and by the love of the Spirit, to strive together with me in your prayers to God for me, that I may be rescued from those who are disobedient in Judea, and that my service for Jerusalem may prove acceptable to the saints" (Romans 15:30–31). Paul encouraged the Roman Christians to strive together with him in prayer to God (v. 30). To struggle in prayer is not necessarily a bad thing, because when we pray with intensity (passion), God listens (see Colossians 4:12; Hebrews 5:7; 1 John 5:13–15).

So how do we strive in prayer? How do we become (more) passionate in prayer? The answer is found, at least in part, in Romans 15:30–33.

First, we become more passionate in prayer when we know God, acknowledging the lordship of Christ and appreciating the love of the Spirit (Romans 15:30). Zeal diminishes (and ceases to exist) without proper motivation. Fervent prayers stem from the knowledge that God is sovereign and merciful. When we consider the grace of God, the forgiveness that He offers, and the intercession that Jesus and the Spirit provide, how can we not be passionate in our communication to the Lord? (see Romans 5:1–5; 8:26–27, 34). So to pray passionately, we must first be passionate about God (Part 1).

Second, we become more passionate in prayer when we know the needs of others (Romans 15:30–31). In Lesson 21, we learned that a prayer offered on behalf of others is called a "petition" (or "intercession"). Romans 15:31 notes several petitions that we can bring to God for others:

- Protection. Whether the request be physical or spiritual, we can ask God to protect others (see 2 Thessalonians 3:2; Matthew 6:13).

- Providence. God wants to give good gifts to people, and He allows us to invoke His providence on others (see 2 Thessalonians 3:1; 3 John 2).
- Pardon. God will not pardon (forgive) others solely because of our prayers, but we can and should pray for their salvation (see Romans 10:1; James 5:16; 1 Timothy 2:1–8).

When we love others and consider all the requests that can be made for them, it will help us to become passionate about interceding on their behalf.

Third, we become more passionate in prayer when we recognize the blessings associated with prayer (Romans 15:32–33). Romans 15:32–33 specifically lists three of these blessings: joy, revival, and peace.

- Joy. The Lord Himself promised His apostles that their joy would be complete when they made requests of Him, and the same is true for us (see John 16:23–24; Romans 15:32).
- Revival. Paul hoped to find refreshment from the Christians in Rome when he visited them, and he acknowledged that this would be the result of their passionate prayers (see Romans 15:32). Similarly, when we pray, we will in one way or another be revived by the Lord (see Ephesians 3:14–16).
- Peace. When we pray passionately to God, bringing our concerns to Him, His peace eliminates our worries, quiets our minds, and envelops our hearts (see Romans 15:33; Philippians 4:6–7).

The dividends connected with passionate prayers are well worth the investment of our time and effort. The results of passionate prayer are phenomenal. Why would anyone want to miss out on these blessings?

Do we long to be passionate in our prayers? This does not happen quickly or easily yet much is gained from it and much lost by failing to do so (see Ephesians 6:12, 18). Knowing God, the needs of others, and the blessings of prayer will help us to become more passionate in prayer.

Pray

Try to commit to at least fourteen minutes of prayer daily this week. Consider beginning with these prayer suggestions.

- **Week 11, Day 5:** Ask God to show you who He is so that you can be more passionate in prayer.
- **Week 11, Day 6:** Promise God that you will spend more time and energy investigating, praying for, and meeting the needs of others.
- **Week 11, Day 7:** Thank God for the joy, revival, and peace that you experience when you pray to Him.

Sing

"A Passion for My God," Glenda Schales

Examine

Do I pray passionately to God? When have I been especially passionate in my prayers? Why was I so engaged at that time(s)? If my prayers have been impersonal and rote, what can I do to be more fervent in prayer today?

_____

_____

_____

_____

Discuss

Answer the following questions. Be ready to discuss them as a group.

1. What does it mean to pray passionately? Is passion strictly an emotion? Explain. How might passionate prayer vary from person to person?

_____

_____

_____

_____

2. Read Romans 15:30–33. Why is it important to pray passionately? How can we become more passionate in prayer? (Feel free to offer additional strategies other than those suggested in the lesson.) Provide biblical examples of passionate prayers.

_____

_____

_____

_____

3. Is it possible to be passionate in prayer yet not be engaged (or effective) in it? (see Romans 10:2) If so, in what way(s), and how can we avoid (or correct) this problem? If not, explain.

_____

_____

_____

_____

LESSON 23 Evangelistic Prayer

"**B**rethren, my heart's desire and my prayer to God for [the Jews] is for their salvation" (Romans 10:1; see 9:1–5). What intensity of feeling! What sincere love for lost souls! Paul wanted his kinsmen to be saved, and he prayed fervently for them. He even went so far as to say that "[he] could wish that [he himself] were accursed, separated from Christ for the sake of [his] brethren, [his] kinsmen according to the flesh" (9:3). Though the Jews still needed to repent, the apostle

interceded for them in prayer. The example of Paul shows us that God listens when we pray for the lost. In fact, Paul urges us to prioritize evangelistic prayer (1 Timothy 2:1–8). (Please read 1 Timothy 2:1–8 before moving forward in the lesson.)

Paul left Timothy in Ephesus to encourage the saints and to combat the error of the Judaizers (see 1 Timothy 1:3–20). In light of the conflicts within and without, Paul urged Timothy and the Ephesian Christians to pray. The phrase *first of all* (2:1) implies that the exhortation to pray is of first importance. What is the first line of defense against false teaching? Prayer. What is the support of Christian unity? Prayer. What is the beginning of evangelism? Prayer. God wants us to be a people of prayer. But He does not want us to pray only for ourselves and other Christians. He wants us to pray for all people—even non-Christians!

What, then, should be the focus of our prayers for non-Christians? The repetition of the words *all* (Gr. *pas*) and *men* (Gr. *antropos*) in 1 Timothy 2:1–8 suggests that the priority of our prayers needs to be evangelistic. We pray for *all men* (1 Timothy 2:1; see v. 2), because God wants to save *all men* (v. 4). There is one mediator between God and *men*, the *man* Jesus Christ (v. 5), who gave Himself as a ransom for *all* people (v. 6). While we should pray about the physical, temporal needs of non-Christians, our chief concern ought to be their salvation. With so much error in the world, evangelistic prayer is indispensable. We need to pray that people will hear and obey the gospel—and that God will use us to teach them. E. M. Bounds rightly observed that "our prayers should be thrown across [the] pathway [of men] as they rush in their downward course to a lost eternity."

To be clear, prayer alone will not save the lost (see Appendix 5). People must come to "the knowledge of the truth" to be saved (v. 4). Praying for the lost will, however, affect our outreach. Evangelistic prayer manifests our conviction that salvation is only in Jesus Christ (vv. 5–6). It acknowledges the lost condition of non-Christians, their ultimate destiny (hell), and our responsibility to them (v. 7). Praying for the lost also motivates us to live holy, influential lives (v. 8). An added benefit of praying for all people—especially for "kings and all who are in authority" (v. 2)—is that it results in a better life for Christians now. Wouldn't the world be a better place if governments were full of true disciples of Jesus?!

How then do we prioritize evangelistic prayer? First, we need to *consider* the lost. Do we ever find ourselves caught up in everyday activities, blind to the spiritual condition of our non-Christian friends and family? We need to acknowledge and interact with lost people. We will not pray for them until we really "see" them. Second, we need to *pray* for the lost. Prayer evidences our belief that God works in our lives and in the lives of others. When we pray for specific people—perhaps having made a (mental or written) list of evangelistic prospects— God will act, because He wants those people to be saved. Third, we need to *watch* for God-given opportunities to teach the lost and then *act*. When we ask God to open doors, we should not be surprised when He does. Instead, we need to take advantage of the opportunities He places before us. Souls are literally at stake!

God wants to save all people regardless of whether we pray for them. Yet He asks us to intercede on behalf of non-Christians so that He can use us to teach them. Do we want to work with God and bring people to Christ? The first step is prayer.

Pray

Try to commit to at least fifteen minutes of prayer daily this week. Consider beginning with these prayer suggestions.

- **Week 12, Day 1:** Praise God that He sent Jesus to save all people.
- **Week 12, Day 2:** Thank God that He has chosen to use you to share the good news with others.
- **Week 12, Day 3:** Ask God to give you opportunities to teach your family, friends, and neighbors. (Be specific about the individuals whom you hope to reach.)
- **Week 12, Day 4:** Promise God that you will be on the lookout for opportunities to tell others about Jesus.

Sing

"Lead Me to Some Soul Today," Will Houghton and Ellis Crum

Examine

Why does God want me to pray for all people? How often do I pray for the lost? What specific individuals do I want to reach with the gospel?

_____

_____

_____

_____

Discuss

Answer the following questions. Be ready to discuss them as a group.

1. Read 1 Timothy 2:1–8. Why does God want us to pray for all people? We can intercede for non-Christians regarding various issues, but what should be our primary focus on their behalf? Have you ever prayed for the lost? Why, and what was the result?

_____

_____

_____

2. Does personal or intercessory prayer alone save non-Christians? Explain. (See Appendix 5.) How does evangelistic prayer affect those who are praying for the lost?

_____

_____

_____

3. Read Colossians 4:2–6. Why did Paul want the Colossians to pray for him? What does this passage teach you about prayer and evangelism? (Optional Assignment: Find other New Testament passages that touch on evangelistic prayer, and discuss their implications and applications for modern Christians.)

_____

_____

_____

_____

LESSON 24 — A Lifelong Commitment Is a Daily Decision

This is not the end. Though we have come to the final lesson in this study, devotion to prayer is not necessarily attained in a few months of shared discussion. It is imperative that we continue to prioritize prayer, individually and collectively.

Hopefully, we now have a stronger commitment to prayer. Yet persistent zeal is needed lest we lose what we have gained. Unfortunately, it is easy to slip back into poor prayer habits. Though not specifically discussing our devotion to prayer, the Bible says, "For this reason we must pay much closer attention to what we have heard, so that we do not drift away from it" (Hebrews 2:1; see also 2 Peter 1:10–11). We typically do not give up on serious commitments overnight; we drift! This does not mean, however, that we are not doomed to failure. We *can* be devoted to prayer for the rest of our lives!

Lifelong devotion to prayer may seem to be a daunting goal, but it is possible. So, how,

practically, do we make this commitment and maintain it? The short answer, we need to make lifelong devotion to prayer a daily decision. There are several reasons why this is helpful.

First, if we approach devotion to prayer with a generalized commitment, we will likely fail. Broad statements, like "I am going to devote myself to prayer for the rest of my life," are noble in sentiment but difficult—if not impossible—to implement. To the above example, we could ask, "When? Where? How?" Without specific strategies in place, resolutions typically fall by the wayside. Winston Churchill (supposedly) said, "He who fails to plan is planning to fail." There is nothing wrong with telling ourselves that we want to be more committed to prayer, but to put it into practice we must make a (daily) plan of action.

Another issue that leads to failed commitment is the expectation of perfection. News flash, we are not perfect! Even after we become Christians, we still do what we should not and do not do what we should (see Romans 7:14–25). There will be times of weakness when we fail to devote ourselves to prayer as we should, and for many of us—especially so-called perfectionists—there will be the temptation to give up altogether after one or two "bad days." God knows that we sin, but instead of allowing us to quit, He encourages us to confess and repent (see 1 John 1:5–10). After failure, it is all the more important that we commit to prayer with renewed vigor.

Lastly, we need to take one day at a time. The Lord Himself said, "So do not worry about tomorrow; for tomorrow will care for itself. Each day has enough trouble of its own" (Matthew 6:34). While Jesus is not discouraging planning for the future, He is stressing the importance of an ever-present faith in God (see v. 33). We are not guaranteed tomorrow. By focusing on daily devotion, we make the most of present opportunities and equip ourselves for the future (see Hebrews 3:12–15; 2 Corinthians 6:1–2). Like Joshua, we must decide *today* that we will serve the Lord: "If it is disagreeable in your sight to serve the LORD, choose for yourselves today whom you will serve: whether the gods which your fathers served which were beyond the River, or the gods of the Amorites in whose land you are living; but as for me and my house, we will serve the LORD" (Joshua 24:15). We must commit to prayer not just once but every day. In this way, we faithfully manage the only time we truly possess (today) and prepare for the future (eternity).

Is lifelong commitment to prayer possible? Yes! With specific planning, realistic expectations, daily devotion, and (most importantly) God's help, we can be devoted to prayer.

We end our study with this question: will *you* devote yourself to prayer?

May the Lord bless you as you do!

Pray

Try to commit to at least fifteen minutes of prayer daily this week. Consider beginning with these prayer suggestions.

- **Week 12, Day 5:** Promise God that you will engage in prayer for the rest of your life by committing to a daily habit of prayer.
- **Week 12, Day 6:** Thank God that He is longsuffering and that He forgives your failed commitments as you confess and repent.
- **Week 12, Day 7:** Ask God to give you the desire and the strength to continue your daily devotion to prayer until you see Him face to face.

Sing

"**Day by Day**," Carolina Sandell-Berg (Trans., Andrew Skoog)

Examine

Have I ever made generic commitments to God that I did not plan specifically to fulfill? In periods of weakness and failure, do I tend to rely on God and try harder, or do I tend to give up altogether? What can I do today to devote myself to prayer?

_____

_____

_____

_____

Discuss

Answer the following questions. Be ready to discuss them as a group.

1. Why is it sometimes difficult to maintain long-term spiritual commitments? What helps motivate you to persevere in spiritual activities (e.g., prayer)?

_____

_____

_____

_____

2. Read 1 Thessalonians 5:17 and Ephesians 6:18. What do the phrases "pray without ceasing" and "pray at all times" mean? How do these phrases relate to the concept of daily and lifelong commitment(s) to prayer? Do these passages encourage or discourage you? Explain.

_____

_____

_____

_____

3. How have you have benefited from this study of prayer? What part influenced you the most? Do you intend to continue praying to God daily? If so, what are you going to do to guarantee that you maintain this commitment?

_____

_____

_____

_____

Appendix 1
Staying Focused in Prayer

The first time this material was taught, this question came up more than once: "How can I stay focused as I am praying? I get distracted easily and am unable to think of things to pray for—especially when I am praying for an extended period of time." No doubt, many of us struggle with prolonged focus in prayer. This problem is exacerbated by our fast-paced, bullet-point culture. What can we do to remedy this and engage more fully in prayer? Though some of the suggestions below have been mentioned in previous lessons, they are included again for continuity and reinforcement.

First, we need to eliminate distractions. We cannot focus on prayer when we are constantly being interrupted and thinking about other things. It is probably best to turn off electronic devices while praying. It is also helpful to find a quiet time and place. It is much harder to focus when and where others are seeking our attention. Jesus often left his disciples and the crowds to pray (see Mark 1:35; 6:46; Luke 6:12). Furthermore, though he was addressing a different issue, Jesus said, "But you, when you pray, go into your inner room, close your door and pray to your Father who is in secret, and your Father who sees what is done in secret will reward you" (Matthew 6:6). To stay focused in prayer, we must eliminate distractions.

Second, we need to develop a routine but allow for spontaneity. Sometimes we have difficulty focusing because we do not plan our prayers. This may stem from the belief that scheduling or planning prayer is less intimate or spiritual. Yet preparing for prayer in advance actually allows us to concentrate. Many of the prayers in the Bible were well-thought-out, poetic compositions (see Psalms). Thus, it is sometimes helpful to have a general outline (a "prayer" list) in mind before we begin praying. Moreover, we should pray when we focus well. Some find that praying first thing in the morning works for them (see Psalm 5:3).

However, our prayers should not become rigid and rehearsed. They should be sincere and intimate. This requires some level of spontaneity. We may plan the timing and content of our prayers, but we need to be ready to change that schedule, take breaks, and alter the subject matter, if the situation warrants. Furthermore, when praying for longer periods of time, being flexible allows us to expand the content of our prayers, to build on previous statements, and to incorporate the requests of others. To stay focused in prayer, we need to plan but not rigidly; thoughtful communication with the Lord occasionally requires spontaneity.

Third, we need to practice focusing—even when we are not praying. Meditation has become a lost art in our current culture. Yet the ability to concentrate is essential, especially for Bible study and prayer. Like other skills, concentration can be learned and practiced. Instead of constantly filling our minds with trivial thoughts from mindless sources (e.g., TV, computer, cell phone), we need to practice thinking on higher things (see Colossians 3:1-2; Psalm 1:2; Philippians 4:8; 1 Timothy 4:15). Then, we will be better prepared to engage fully in prayer (see Psalms 5:1-2; 19:14). To stay focused in prayer, we must practice staying focused.

Fourth, we need to determine what methods work best for us. Some focus better when they write out (or type) their prayers in a prayer journal. Others thrive when they use the written prayers of others for inspiration (e.g., devotional guides, hymns, Scripture). Some need a prayer list, while others do not. Some focus when they have a general outline for prayer (e.g., A.C.T.S.), but others prefer spontaneity. (The A.C.T.S. outline is Adoration, Confession, Thanksgiving, and Supplication.) Some do well with their eyes closed; others open. Some concentrate best when they pray silently, while others need to pray out loud. We can explore any scriptural strategy. The goal is to find something that keeps us engaged in prayer. To stay focused in prayer, we must find a method that works.

Learning what keeps us focused in prayer can be intimidating at first but soon proves to be an exciting endeavor. Personal evaluation and a willingness to change are vital, but we will be the better for it. If the suggestions above help you, use them. When you try something new, however, make sure to reflect on it and adjust as needed. The aim is not just to stay focused on a prayer but to connect with God. Let's keep this ultimate goal before us always.

To God be the glory!

Appendix 2
Let the People Say "Amen"

A practice common to Jews, Christians, and Muslims is the saying of "Amen" at key points in worship, frequently at the close of prayers. But what does *amen* mean? Is the practice biblical? If so, is it required, or is it optional? Who should say "Amen," and why?

First of all, *amen* is a Hebrew word. It is found throughout the Old Testament. It was transliterated into Greek for the New Testament and later into Latin and English. The basic meaning of the word, when it is used as an adjective, is "faithful" or "sure." *Amen* describes God (see Deuteronomy 7:9; Isaiah 49:7; 65:16), His word (see Psalms 19:7; 111:7), and His works (see Hosea 5:9; Isaiah 33:16; 55:3). It is also used of people (see Proverbs 11:13; 25:13). *Amen* can be used as an adverb meaning "truly" or "certainly" (see Matthew 16:28; Luke 9:27) or as a noun meaning "yes" (Revelation 1:7; 22:20).

In the Bible, when God uses *amen*, it carries the idea of "thus it shall be" (see Matthew 5:18). When it is used by people, *amen* means "let it be so" (see Revelation 22:20). The interpretation "let it be so" is strengthened in the Septuagint (the Greek translation of the Old Testament). The Septuagint typically translates the Hebrew *amen* with the Greek *genoito*, which means "may it be" (see Numbers 5:22; Luke 1:28; Romans 3:4).

The word *amen* is used in the Old Testament by individuals and groups to agree with statements, to acknowledge blessings or penalties, and to vow obedience (see Deuteronomy 27:15–28; Jeremiah 11:5; Nehemiah 5:13). It is used as a response in praise of God, admitting the truthfulness of a statement and accepting it as one's own (see 1 Chronicles 16:36; Nehemiah 8:6; Psalms 41:13; 72:19; 89:52; 106:48).

In the intertestamental period, *amen* was the response of the synagogue to the praises and blessings pronounced by the leader. The rabbis of this period saw great value in saying "Amen." They wrote, "Greater is he who responds 'Amen' than he who blesses," and "Whoever answers 'Amen,' his name shall be great and blessed, and the decree of his damnation is utterly done away;" they also wrote, "To him who answers 'Amen' the gates of Paradise are open" (Marvin R. Vincent).

In the New Testament, the word *amen* is introduced by Jesus, and in the Gospels, He alone says it. It is typically translated as "truly" or "verily." Jesus often places it before His sayings (30x in Matthew, 13x in Mark, 6x in Luke, and 50x in John—though it is liturgically doubled in John). *Amen* even becomes a designation of Jesus Himself, demonstrating that He is the fulfillment of all the promises of God (see 2 Corinthians 1:20; Revelation 3:14).

Another use of *amen* in the New Testament—and the one that most readily touches our practice—is the use of *amen* as a verbal affirmation. The custom of first-century Christians was to say "Amen" following praises of God, prayers to Him, and statements of truth about Him and His word—just as in the Old Testament (see 1 Corinthians 14:16; Ephesians 3:21; Galatians 6:18; Revelation 22:20). Thus, Paul wrote not just of an Amen but the Amen in 1 Corinthians 14:16, signaling that it was a typical practice in the church.

After the first century, this custom continued in liturgies. In fact, Jerome, a fourth-century historian, noted that "the united 'Amen' of the people sounded like the fall of water or the sound of thunder." (Does that describe our contemporary practice? Oh that it did!)

The Amen is a biblically authorized and historically sanctioned practice, but when should we say "Amen" today? We learn from divinely approved examples that there are several occasions when saying "Amen" is appropriate. Perhaps the most suitable time to say it is at the close of our collective prayers (see 1 Corinthians 14:16).

Who should say "Amen"? The Bible implies that any Christian—male or female—who wholeheartedly agrees with what has been said can and should say the Amen. Some question whether a woman can say "Amen" in the assemblies. Though the Bible instructs women to be silent in church, the Amen—like singing and confession—does not seem to violate their divinely appointed role (see 1 Corinthians 14:34–35; 1 Timothy 2:11–12).

Saying "Amen" follows the pattern of Scripture, encourages participation in prayer, adds energy to the assemblies, and glorifies God. The Bible says, "Blessed be the LORD, the God of Israel, / From everlasting even to everlasting. / And let all the people say, 'Amen.' / Praise the LORD!" (Psalm 106:48). Will we answer the call? Who among us will say "Amen"?

Appendix 3
Prayer and Fasting

Fasting is an uncommon activity in our modern, Western culture. People tend to associate it with cultic and Eastern religions, ancient mysticism, medieval monasticism, or non-traditional health management. Obviously, there are misconceptions about fasting. Yet the Bible portrays fasting as an acceptable and spiritually beneficial practice. Biblical fasting is typically linked with prayer. In this study, we will survey the nature and application of fasting in the Bible and its relevance today.

In the Old Testament, several Hebrew and Aramaic words relate to fasting. These include the Hebrew verb *tsum*, meaning "to fast" (that is, "to abstain from food"), and the noun *tsom*, meaning "fast(ing)." Another Hebrew word *nazar* (verb) is sometimes translated as "to abstain" but fundamentally means "to consecrate"; it is the root of the word *Nazarite*; interestingly, Nazarites were to abstain from various kinds of drinks (see Numbers 6:2–3). The Hebrew words *taanith* (noun) and *anah* (verb) are also indirectly linked to fasting; these words mean "humiliation" and "to humble oneself" and, by implication from certain contexts, "through fasting." Lastly, the Aramaic word *tevath* is translated "fasting" and seems to convey the idea of "twisting in hunger."

In the New Testament, the Greek words are nearly identical in meaning to the Hebrew and Aramaic. The Greek verb *nesteuo* means "to fast"; there seems to be more of a religious connotation attached to this word than to its Hebrew counterparts. The root of this verb is the Greek adjective *nestis*, which simply means "hungry." Finally, the Greek noun *nesteia* means "fast" and describes voluntary or forced abstinence from food.

Regardless of the word that is used, fasting is simply abstaining from food—typically for spiritual reasons. (More on the reasons for fasting below.)

Examples of fasting abound in the Scriptures. In the Old Testament, Moses fasted for a period of forty days and nights while he received the Law (Exodus 34:28). The Israelites fasted during times of war (Judges 20:26; 1 Samuel 7:6). They also fasted for seven days following the death of King Saul (1 Samuel 31:13). David fasted and prayed for his sick child (2 Samuel 12:16; see Psalm 35:13). Jehoshaphat fasted when threatened by Edom (2 Chronicles 20:3). Ezra fasted before a dangerous journey, asking God for safe travels (Ezra 8:21). Nehemiah fasted and prayed after he heard that Jerusalem was lying in ruins (Nehemiah 1:4). Esther and the Jews fasted after they learned of their imminent annihilation (Esther 4:3, 16). Joel called for a communal fast during a pestilence (Joel 1:14; 2:15). The Ninevites held a city-wide fast in response to the preaching of Jonah (Jonah 3:5–9).

In the New Testament, Anna fasted regularly (Luke 2:37). Jesus began His ministry with a forty-day fast (Matthew 4:2). The disciples of John fasted often, and it is implied that the disciples of Jesus would do the same when it was appropriate (Matthew 9:14–15; see 6:16–18). Cornelius fasted and prayed to God, and an angel was sent to him in response (Acts 10:30). As the early Christians ministered to the Lord and made important decisions, they also fasted (Acts 13:2; 14:23). Fasting was obviously a common and valued practice among God's people.

Yet the fasts in the Bible are not identical. Sometimes fasting was natural because food was unavailable or because individuals were grief-stricken (see 2 Corinthians 6:5; 11:27; 2 Samuel 1:11–12). The extent and duration of fasts were typically determined by the individual (or the group) and were contingent on the immediate circumstances.

Some fasts were partial, removing only certain items from the diet (see Daniel 10:2–3; 1:12); normal fasts, on the other hand, abstained from all food but allowed the drinking of water (see Luke 4:2, 4); the extreme total fast, however, refrained from food and drink altogether (see Acts 9:9; Esther 4:15–16). The fasts of the Bible also varied in length: one day (see Judges 20:26), three days (see Esther 4:16), seven days (see 1 Samuel 31:13), or even forty days (see Exodus 34:28). The particulars of fasting were rarely mandated in Scripture.

Fasting is clearly not an isolated or rare activity in the Bible. It is not specifically commanded in the New Testament but was important to first-century believers. So why does it seem that fasting is frequently ignored by modern Christians? Perhaps it is because we simply do not recognize its value (or because we have not spent time learning about it).

What, then, are some of the spiritual benefits of fasting?

First and foremost, fasting intensifies our prayers. Let's consider the example of Daniel. While seeking an explanation of Jeremiah's prophecy, Daniel wrote, "So I gave my attention to the Lord God to seek Him by prayer and supplications, with fasting, sackcloth and ashes" (Daniel 9:3). Daniel wanted God to know that he was serious about approaching Him, so he fasted. Similar stories include Ahab (1 Kings 21:27), Ezra (Ezra 8:23) and Paul (Acts 9:9). In the Bible, desperate times called for desperate measures, and fasting was sometimes deemed necessary. Moreover, fasting adds fervency to prayer (see James 5:16). It humbles us (see Ezra 8:21; Psalm 35:13) and teaches us self-control (see 1 Corinthians 7:5). Fasting demonstrates our reliance on the Lord (see 2 Chronicles 20:3). It meets His approval (see Matthew 6:18). Great rewards are therefore associated with fasting, especially when it is coupled with prayer.

Can we fast today? Yes, we can. Should we? That is an individual decision that requires awareness of oneself and his or her circumstances. We need to identify our motivations and determine how effective fasting will be for us personally. If we simply want to try something new and different, we may be disappointed with fasting. But if we recognize the spiritual benefits associated with fasting, it may prove profitable. Regardless, if we fast, we must do so only to the glory of God (see Zechariah 7:5; Matthew 6:17–18). When we do so, God will reward us.

Appendix 4
Praying in the Holy Spirit

There is much confusion among professed Christians regarding the person and work of the Holy Spirit. As it relates to our discussion of prayer, differences abound concerning the connection between the Spirit and our prayers. There are only a few times in the Bible that the specific phrase *praying in the Holy Spirit*—or something nearly identical to it—is used (Jude 20; Ephesians 6:18; 1 Corinthians 14:15), and these occurrences contain interpretive challenges that result in disagreements. So, what does it mean to pray in the Spirit?

First, we need to examine the primary passages in their contexts. The exact phrase is *praying in the Holy Spirit* is used in Jude 20: "But you, beloved, building yourselves up on your most holy faith, praying in the Holy Spirit, keep yourselves in the love of God, waiting anxiously for the mercy of our Lord Jesus Christ to eternal life" (vv. 20–21). In the context, Jude is accusing false teachers of being "devoid of the Spirit," referring to their lack of spirituality (v. 19). In contrast, Jude instructs the believers to pray in the Holy Spirit. The false teachers are condemned for their descent into the lower human nature, and the phrase *praying in the Holy Spirit* implies believers need to pray according to the higher nature of the Spirit (see 1 Corinthians 2:10–16; Colossians 3:1–2).

A similar phrase is found in Ephesians 6:18: "With all prayer and petition pray at all times in the Spirit, and with this in view, be on the alert with all perseverance and petition for all the saints." Unlike the previous example, the adjective *holy* is missing, allowing for the possibility that this passage does not deal with the Holy Spirit directly but with the human spirit (see 1 Corinthians 14:14). It seems, however, in view of Paul's use of the phrase *in the Spirit* in Ephesians, that the Holy Spirit and His influence are in view (see 2:22; 3:5; 5:18). The exhortation, then, is to pray as directed by the Spirit. This does not necessarily refer to inspired prayers but to prayers that match what the Spirit has revealed (see Ephesians 6:17; 5:18; Colossians 3:16.)

The final passage that corresponds with the phrase *praying in the Holy Spirit* is 1 Corinthians 14:15, which says, "What is the outcome then? I will pray with the spirit and I will pray with the mind also; I will sing with the spirit and I will sing with the mind also." This is a difficult passage. The context addresses the use (and misuse) of miraculous spiritual gifts, including praying in tongues (see 1 Corinthians 12:1; 14:14). Though many consider the Spirit in verse 15 to be the human spirit, it seems better to view this as a reference to the Holy Spirit. (For more on this debate, compare commentaries on 1 Corinthians.) Consequently, this passage has limited application today because the ability to pray in tongues has ceased (see 1 Corinthians 13:8). However, the principle remains—prayer is associated with the Spirit's influence.

Second, we need to compare the passages that speak directly of praying in the Spirit with those that address it indirectly. Praying in the Spirit relates to the Spirit's participation in our adoption by God. The Bible says, "Because you are sons, God has sent forth the Spirit of His Son into our hearts, crying, 'Abba! Father!'" (Galatians 4:6; see Ephesians 2:18). Prayer is possible because the Spirit has effected our spiritual rebirth and adoption (see John 3:5; Titus

3:5). The Spirit Himself, therefore, cries out to God on our behalf.

The intercession of the Spirit is always available to us, even when we are weak. The Bible says, "In the same way the Spirit also helps our weakness; for we do not know how to pray as we should, but the Spirit Himself intercedes for us with groanings too deep for words; and He who searches the hearts knows what the mind of the Spirit is, because He intercedes for the saints according to the will of God" (Romans 8:25-26). What a comfort to know that the Spirit helps us when we pray to God! The Holy Spirit gives us access to God, affirms our sonship, and overcomes our inadequacies.

To sum up, praying in the Spirit means simply that we pray in accordance with what the Spirit has revealed to us (and about us) in the Scriptures. J. Oswald Sanders was right when he said, "It hardly need be said that to pray in the Spirit means to pray in harmony with the Word of God, which He has inspired. He does not speak with two voices." If the Spirit of God dwells in us, we will be in sync with Him, living and praying as He desires. As J. Stuart Holden concludes, "Praying in the Holy Ghost is but cooperating with the will of God, and such prayer is always victorious."

Appendix 5
Calling on the Name of the Lord

"**E**veryone who calls on the name of the Lord will be saved." This promise is found throughout the Bible and intends to instill within us hope that God can and will save us, if we turn to Him. Yet among professed Christians, this statement is a source of great confusion and debate. Many affirm that calling on the name of the Lord only involves faith, repentance, and prayer—specifically the Sinner's Prayer. Is this what the Bible teaches? What does it really mean to call on the name of the Lord?

Calling on the name of the Lord is not merely a New Testament concept. It is actually rooted in the Old Testament, first mentioned in Genesis 4:26. Faithful individuals (e.g., Abraham, David, and Elijah) called on the Lord for salvation and blessing and in worship (see Genesis 12:8; Psalm 18:6; 1 Kings 18:24). Yet this was not simply making a request. It required seeking God, forsaking evil, and returning to the Lord (see Isaiah 55:6; Jeremiah 29:12–13). It meant doing whatever God desired.

The New Testament continues with this same understanding but refines it in view of the gospel of the Lord Jesus. The Bible does not teach that a so-called Sinner's Prayer is the way to salvation. In fact, the Sinner's Prayer—as it is typically taught today—is found nowhere in the Old and New Testaments. Rather, the Bible says we are forgiven of our sins by the grace of God through obedient faith in the Lord (see Ephesians 2:8; Hebrews 5:9).

So how do we call on the name of the Lord today? There are two passages in the New Testament that explicitly state that "everyone who calls on the name of the Lord will be saved" (Acts 2:21; Romans 10:13). In Romans 10, we learn that calling on the name of the Lord includes various activities associated with faith: (1) hearing and believing the word of Christ (vv. 14–17) and (2) believing and confessing the lordship of Jesus (vv. 8–12). From this passage, we can begin to outline what it means to call on the name of the Lord: "Everyone who calls on the name of the Lord will be saved" = Everyone who hears, believes, and confesses the name of Jesus will be saved.

But, the New Testament does not end with the teaching of Romans 10. Acts 2 further defines the expectations associated with calling on the name of the Lord, incorporating (1) repentance and (2) baptism (vv. 21, 38). It is worth noting that there is a verbal connection between calling *on the name of the Lord* (v. 21) and being baptized *in* (literally, *on*) *the name of Jesus Christ* (v. 38). Putting Romans 10 and Acts 2 together: "Everyone who calls on the name of the Lord will be saved" = Everyone who hears, believes, confesses, repents, and is baptized in the name of Jesus will be saved.

Though many reject the necessity of baptism, it is precisely at this point that God has determined that we are calling on Him for salvation. The Bible says, "Now why do you delay? Get up and be baptized, and wash away your sins, calling on Him name" (Acts 22:16; see 1 Peter 3:21; Romans 6:3–4; Mark 16:16). Everyone who calls on the name of the Lord will be saved. Yet, sadly, one who has not heard, believed, repented, confessed, and been baptized has not called on his name and has not been saved.

The question, therefore, comes to you and to me: "Have I called on the name of the Lord?"

Works Consulted

"Amazing Grace." Wikipedia. https://en.wikipedia.org/wiki/Amazing_Grace.

Blomberg, Craig L., and Jennifer Foutz Markley. *A Handbook of New Testament Exegesis.* Grand Rapids: Baker Academic, 2010.

Bruce, F. F. *The Epistle to the Galatians: A Commentary on the Greek Text.* NIGTC. Grand Rapids: Eerdmans, 1982.

"Casual." Dictionary.com. http://www.dictionary.com/browse/casual.

Danker, Frederick W., Walter Bauer, William F. Arndt, and F. Wilbur Gingrich. *Greek-English Lexicon of the New Testament and Other Early Christian Literature.* 3rd ed. Chicago: University of Chicago Press, 2000.

"Faith." Dictionary.com. http://www.dictionary.com/browse/faith.

"Friedrich Nietzsche." Wikiquote. https://simple.wikiquote.org/wiki/Friedrich_Nietzsche.

Hamilton, Clinton. *1 Peter.* Truth Commentaries. Bowling Green, KY: Guardian of Truth Foundation, 1995.

———. *2 Peter and Jude.* Truth Commentaries. Bowling Green, KY: Guardian of Truth Foundation, 1995.

"Hezekiah." Bible Odyssey. https://www.bibleodyssey.org/HarperCollinsBibleDictionary/h/hezekiah.

Holladay, William L., ed. *A Concise Hebrew and Aramaic Lexicon of the Old Testament.* Grand Rapids: Eerdmans, 1988.

Ingram, Chip. *God as He Longs for You to See Him.* Grand Rapids: Baker Books, 2004.

Kendrick, Stephen, and Alex Kendrick. *The Battle Plan for Prayer: From Basic Training to Targeted Strategies.* Nashville: B&H Publishing, 2015.

Kittel, Gerhard, and Gerhard Friedrich, eds. *Theological Dictionary of the New Testament.* Translated by Geoffrey W. Bromiley. 10 vols. Grand Rapids: Eerdmans, 1964–1976.

Mounce, William D., ed. *Mounce's Complete Expository Dictionary of Old and New Testament Words.* Grand Rapids: Zondervan, 2006.

"Narcissus (mythology)." Wikipedia. https://en.wikipedia.org/wiki/Narcissus_(mythology).

Packer, J. I. *Knowing God.* Downers Grove: InterVarsity Press, 1993.

"Prayer." Dictionary.com. http://www.dictionary.com/browse/prayer.

Riemann, Paul A. *Dissonant Pieties: John Calvin and the Prayer Psalms of the Psalter.* Eugene, OR: Cascade, 2013.

Robertson, A. T. *Word Pictures in the New Testament.* New York: Richard R. Smith, 1930.

Rowell, Edward K., ed. *1001 Quotes, Illustrations, and Humorous Stories for Preachers, Teachers, and Writers.* Grand Rapids: Baker Books, 2007.

Sanders, J. Oswald. *Prayer Power Unlimited.* Grand Rapids: Discovery House, 1997.

———. *Spiritual Leadership.* Basingstoke: Marshall Pickering, 1986.

Slater-Robins, Max. "15 Inspirational Quotes from Steve Jobs." Business Insider. http://www.businessinsider.com/steve-jobs-quotes-life-advice-2015-9.

Swindoll, Charles, R. *Swindoll's Ultimate Book of Illustrations & Quotes.* Nashville: Nelson, 1998.

Thielman, Frank. *Theology of the New Testament.* Grand Rapids: Zondervan, 2005.

Tozer, A. W. *The Attributes of God Volume 1 With Study Guide.* Camp Hill, PA: WingSpread, 2003.

———. *The Attributes of God Volume 2 with Study Guide.* Camp Hill, PA: WingSpread, 2003.

———. *The Knowledge of the Holy.* San Francisco: HarperOne, 2009.

Vincent, Marvin R. *Word Studies in the New Testament.* New York: Scribner, 1887.

Vine, W. E., Merrill F. Unger, and William White, Jr. *Vine's Complete Expository Dictionary of Old and New Testament Words.* Nashville: Nelson, 1984.

Wesley, John. *How to Pray: The Best of John Wesley on Prayer.* Uhrichsville, OH: Barbour, 2007.

Willis, Mike. *First Corinthians.* Truth Commentaries. Bowling Green, KY: Guardian of Truth Foundation, 1994.